# AIP STANDARD CODE OF PARLIAMENTARY PROCEDURE

# WORKBOOK

A workbook for users of
*American Institute of Parliamentarians
Standard Code of
Parliamentary Procedure*

Original Questions compiled by Alice N. Pohl, CPP-T
Revised 2002 by James Lochrie, CPP-T

Revised and Expanded 2014 for
*AIP Standard Code of Parliamentary Procedure*

by
Barry Glazer, CPP-T, Mary L. Randolph, CPP-T,
Mary L. Remson, CPP-T, and Ann L. Rempel, CPP-T

## American Institute of Parliamentarians
Education Department
2014

© 2014, 2015 by American Institute of Parliamentarians
www.aipparl.org
aip@aipparl.org
(888) 664-0428

Produced in the United States of America
ISBN: 978-0-942736-36-6

Second printing January 2015
2 3 4 5 6 7 8 9 10

Produced by the
Education Department
American Institute of Parliamentarians
Jeanette N. Williams, CP-T, Education Director
Ann Rempel, CPP-T, Printed Materials Division Chair
Alison Wallis, CP-T, President

# Acknowledgments

The AIP Education Department acknowledges Alice N. Pohl, CPP-T, who produced a similar workbook based on the *Standard Code of Parliamentary Procedure* written by Alice Sturgis. The department also acknowledges the work of James Lochrie, CPP-T, who contributed his knowledge and time to a 2002 workbook, which updated the work by Alice Pohl.

The department is grateful to the authors of this workbook: Barry Glazer, CPP-T, Mary L. Randolph, CPP-T, Mary Remson, CPP-T, and Ann L. Rempel, CPP-T. Each served on the authorship team for *American Institute of Parliamentarians Standard Code of Parliamentary Procedure (AIPSC)*, McGraw-Hill, 2012.

In addition, the department is grateful to Kay Crews, CP, who spent many hours putting this book into correct order and proper format.

This page intentionally left blank.

# Contents

# INTRODUCTION

## The Philosophy

*American Institute of Parliamentarians Standard Code of Parliamentary Procedure (AIPSC)* is based on the philosophy and writings of Alice Sturgis. The philosophy of Alice Sturgis as it relates to parliamentary law is summed up in her own words in the preface to the first edition of her book[1]:

> The purpose of parliamentary law is to assist an assembly in carrying out its purposes. It is the code of ethics of working together — the rules of the game. Parliamentary law is concerned with the means by which beliefs and ideas are best translated into effective group action. It must provide orderly ways of determining the will of the majority. It must be clear, considerate, kind, fair and it must effect the desired aims of the assembly. It must, in other words, be democratic.

In another part of the preface, she discusses the principles that make the code "completely usable and modern." Her philosophy is based on simplicity, clarity, and conciseness. Her writings in parliamentary law are clear and concise, and her use of modern language and the removal of extraneous rules for motions make her books "completely usable and modern." These principles are embodied in *AIPSC*.

In summary, the philosophy of *AIPSC* is: A parliamentary authority should be so clear and simple that anyone can understand it. The parliamentary authority should be based on invariable principles and common procedures in actual use.

---

[1] *Sturgis Standard Code of Parliamentary Procedure*, Sturgis, Alice F., McGraw-Hill Book Company, Inc. (1950)

The basic principles of parliamentary law are:

1. Parliamentary procedure is to facilitate the orderly transaction of business and to promote cooperation and harmony.
2. Individual persons have the right to associate with other persons to promote and pursue their common interests and aspirations.
3. Individual persons have a right to assemble to promote their common interest.
4. All members have equal rights, privileges, and obligations.
5. The majority vote decides.
6. The rights of the minority must be protected.
7. Full and free discussion of every proposition presented for decision is an established right of members.
8. Every member has the right to know the meaning of the question before the assembly and what its effect will be.
9. All meetings must be characterized by fairness and good faith

## AIPSC Concepts and Rules

This workbook is dedicated to learning the concepts and the rules in *AIPSC*.

To understand the concepts and rules in *AIPSC*, questions are posed on various concepts and rules. This is done chapter by chapter, and will permit the student of *AIPSC* to readily progress through the book, to locate the key words in the question, to read the relevant paragraphs, to analyze and to understand each concept or rule. In some cases, if the answer to the question is not clear, it may become clearer as the student progresses through subsequent questions.

References and answers are also provided at the end of the workbook, but students are urged to do their own research and analysis and to use the references and answers as a last resort.

Students can set the pace at which they study *AIPSC* but should set a timetable for answering the question in each chapter. Perhaps it is two chapters per week, perhaps only one chapter per week. Whatever the pace, the student should try to absorb most concepts and rules before moving to the next chapter.

Having answered all questions in each chapter, the student will have gained an excellent fund of knowledge in *AIPSC* and should be able to put that knowledge to good use.

This page intentionally left blank.

# SECTION 1
# CONCEPTS AND RULES IN *AIPSC*

Find the specific reference in *AIPSC* for each statement or question; write down the page reference and your answer to the question. You may check the answer in Section 2 of this book when the answers have been completed for each chapter.

This page intentionally left blank.

# CHAPTER 1
## Parliamentary Law

1. What are two main historical purposes of "the rules of proceeding"?

2. Name some of the procedural safeguards found in law.

3. What are the procedures available to members to complain when procedure is not followed in a meeting, and to further complain when they believe the presiding officer is unfair or incorrect?

4. What are some of the underlying principles for the rules of debate?

5. What is the purpose of meeting procedures?

6. Where can meeting procedures be found?

7. What is the relationship of customary procedure and written rules of procedure?

8. What rules constitute "parliamentary law"?



9. Give one or more examples of an abuse of parliamentary law.



10. What should be done about tactics that abuse the use of parliamentary law?



11. Name several kinds of organizations that use parliamentary law.



12. Why might the meetings of organizations be required to use parliamentary law?



13. What is the difference in procedure between large organizations and small organizations?



14. What is a parliamentary authority?



15. What are the rules called that are adopted by the organization to supersede the parliamentary authority?



16. Why might an organization choose to adopt special rules to supersede the parliamentary authority?

# CHAPTER 2
## Fundamental Principles of Parliamentary Law

1. What is the purpose of parliamentary law?

2. For what purposes should parliamentary procedure not be used?

3. What are two of the basic procedural rules to ensure the simplest and most direct procedure for accomplishing a purpose?

4. What are the fundamental rights of all people and all members?

5. What should the presiding officer do in regard to equality of the members' rights?

6. What is the ultimate authority of an organization vested in?

7. By joining an organization, a member agrees to be governed by _____.

8.    What are the rights of members?


9.    John Hatsell in 1776 wrote, "Motives ought to outweigh objections of form." What did he mean?

# CHAPTER 3
## Classification of Motions

1.  How are motions classified into groups?

2.  What is the purpose of a main motion?

3.  What are the six main motions that have specific names and are governed by somewhat different rules?

4.  Define subsidiary motions.

5.  What are the most frequently used subsidiary motions?

6.  Define privileged motions.

7.  Name the privileged motions.

8.  Define incidental motions.

9.  Name the incidental motions.

10. What other motions may be made?

11. What subsidiary, privileged, and incidental motions may be main motions if proposed when no main motion is pending?

12. Name at least two features of incidental motions.

13. Because of their nature some incidental motions have two other distinguishing features. Name them.

14. A main motion is pending and a member moves, "that we take the vote by roll call." What type of motion is this?

15. A member moves to table the pending main motion until 3 p.m. How should the presiding officer handle such a motion?

16. If a subsidiary or privileged motion is stated when no other motions are pending, what classification is the motion?

# CHAPTER 4
## Ranking of Motions

1.   What does the rank or precedence of a motion determine?

2.   Name the privileged motions from the highest to the lowest ranking in order of precedence.

3.   Name the subsidiary motions from the highest to the lowest ranking in order of precedence.

4.   What rank do incidental motions have?

5.   What are the two basic rules of ranking?

6.   A main motion has been moved, followed by a motion to refer to a committee. A member wishes to amend the main motion. Would this be permitted?

7.   A main motion is moved, followed by a motion to table. What motions would now be in order?

8.  A main motion, the motion to amend, the motion to limit debate, and the motion to recess are pending. Which motions would now be in order?

9.  Define a pending motion or question.

10. What is meant by the immediately pending motion or question?

# CHAPTER 5
## Rules Governing Motions

1.  What are the nine rules you need to know about each motion?

2.  What two types of motions can interrupt a speaker?

3.  What motions require a second? What are the exceptions?

4.  Are all motions debatable?

5.  Can all motions be amended?

6.  What vote do motions require?

7.  Explain the ranking (precedence) of motions.

8.  To what other motions can motions apply?

9. Can a motion be renewed?


10. What is repeal by implication?

# CHAPTER 6
## Processing of Motions

1.   What is a motion?



2.   What are the steps in presenting a motion?



3.   When a member addresses the presiding officer, what does it indicate?



4.   How is the presiding officer addressed?



5.   How does the presiding officer recognize a member?



6.   When a member seeking the floor does not obtain it, what does the member do?



7.   How must a motion be proposed?



8.   If a member says, "Madam President, I suggest that ...," what should the presiding officer say?

9.  If a member has a lengthy, complicated, or important motion, how should the member submit the motion?

10. What does a second indicate?

11. If there is no second what does the presiding officer say?

12. If a member objects to the lack of a second, what does the presiding officer do?

13. Name two situations where a second is not required.

14. Which is the legal motion, the one stated by the chair or the one stated by a member?

15. When a motion has been properly moved and seconded, what does the presiding officer say?

16. When is a motion called a 'pending question' or a 'pending motion'?

17. What are the seven steps in voting on a motion?

18. Why does the presiding officer restate the pending motion before any other steps in voting?

19. How are the affirmative and negative votes taken?

20. Should the presiding officer always take the negative vote, even if it appears that the affirmative vote is unanimous?

21. What should the presiding officer do if uncertain of which side prevailed in any vote?

22. May some or all of the steps in processing a motion be skipped or combined?

This page intentionally left blank.

# CHAPTER 7
## Main Motions

1.  What is a main motion?

2.  How should a main motion be phrased?

3.  What types of main motions are usually in resolution form?

4.  What is the form of a resolution?

5.  When may discussion of a motion or resolution begin?

6.  What are some of the ways in which disposition of a main motion may occur?

7.  May another main motion on the same subject be proposed while a main motion is pending?

8.  Discuss how a main motion may or may not be renewed when adopted or defeated.

9.    What is the effect of adopting the main motion?


10.    What are the basic rules governing the main motion?

# CHAPTER 8
## Specific Main Motions

1.  What is the purpose of the motion to adopt in-lieu-of?

2.  What happens when a main motion proposed for adoption in lieu of one or more other     main motions is adopted?

3.  What happens when a main motion proposed for adoption in lieu of one or more other main motions is defeated?

4.  What are the basic rules governing a motion to adopt in-lieu-of? Which are different than the rules governing an original (substantive) main motion?

5.  What is the purpose of a motion to amend a previous action?

6.  What previous actions can be amended?

7.  Does the motion to amend a previous action affect actions that have already been taken as a result of the previous action?

8.  What are the basic rules governing the motion to amend a previous action? Which are different than the rules governing an original (substantive) main motion?

9.  Explain the purpose of the motion to ratify.

10.  Why might a motion to ratify be needed?

11.  What are the basic rules governing the motion to ratify? Which are different than the rules governing an original (substantive) main motion?

12.  What is the purpose of the motion to recall a motion or subject from a committee (or board)?

13.  Why might a motion to recall be needed?

14.  What is the effect of adopting a motion to recall?

15. What are the rules governing the motion to recall a motion or subject from a committee (or board)? Which are different than the rules governing an original (substantive) main motion?

16. What is the purpose of the motion to reconsider?

17. What votes can be reconsidered?

18. When can the motion to reconsider be offered? When is a decision on the motion made?

19. Who can move to reconsider?

20. What is the effect of adopting the motion to reconsider?

21. What are the basic rules governing the motion to reconsider? Which are different than the rules governing an original (substantive) main motion?

22. What is the purpose of the motion to rescind?

23. What is the form of the motion to rescind?

24.    What motions may be rescinded?

25.    If a member believes the motion to be rescinded might be
       kept with some changes, can the motion to be rescinded be
       amended instead?

26.    What vote and notice are required to rescind?

27.    What is the effect of adoption of a motion to rescind?

28.    What are the basic rules governing the motion to rescind?
       Which are different than the rules governing an original
       (substantive) main motion?

# CHAPTER 9
## Subsidiary Motions

1. What is the purpose of the motion to amend?

2. What are the four types of amendments?

3. What motions may be amended?

4. What is meant by the phrase "must be germane"?

5. What is a hostile amendment? Are hostile amendments in order?

6. What are the limitations on pending amendments?

7. Are amendments debatable?

8. What does an amendment by substitution do?

9.   How many amendments can a substitution of a new motion have?

10.  Explain how a motion or resolution may be amended by filling blanks.

11.  When can an amendment be withdrawn?

12.  Explain the process by which someone may suggest a change in wording to a motion that has been proposed, without actually moving to amend it.

13.  What does it mean to have "adhering amendments?"

14.  Explain the method of voting on amendments.

15.  What is the vote required for adoption of an amendment?

16.  How can action already taken be amended?

17.  What is the effect of adoption of the motion to amend?

18.    What are the basic rules governing the motion to amend?

19.    What is the purpose of a motion to refer to a committee?

20.    What provisions may be included in the motion to refer?

21.    If a motion is made to refer a subject to a committee, and no main motion is pending, what kind of motion is this?

22.    What is the effect of adoption of the motion to refer?

23.    What are the basic rules governing the motion to refer?

24.    What is the purpose of a motion to postpone to a certain time?

25.    What are the limitations on a motion to postpone to a certain time?

26.    What are some different ways in which a motion may be postponed to a certain time?

27. When a motion is postponed to a later meeting, when is it considered?

28. What happens to a motion that is postponed, but is not taken up at the time or meeting to which it is postponed?

29. What is the effect of adoption of the motion to postpone to a certain time?

30. What are the basic rules governing the motion to postpone to a certain time?

31. What is the purpose of a motion to limit or extend debate?

32. What are the types of limitations that are usually placed on debate?

33. What pending motions are affected by the motion to limit or extend debate?

34. When is the effect of the motion to limit or extend debate terminated?

35. What are the basic rules governing the motion to limit debate?

36. What is the purpose of a motion to close debate and vote immediately?

37. What are some of the restrictions on proposing the motion to close debate and vote immediately?

38. How does the motion to close debate and vote immediately affect pending motions?

39. What is the effect of adoption of the motion to close debate and vote immediately when qualified to apply to more than just the immediately pending motion?

40. How should the presiding officer handle a member who calls out "Call the question" or "Question!"?

41. What are the basic rules governing the motion to close debate and vote immediately?

42. What is the purpose of a motion to table?

43.	What are the reasons that an assembly may wish to table a main motion?

44.	What happens to adhering motions if a main motion is tabled?

45.	If the assembly wishes to reverse the disposal of the main motion, what may the assembly do?

46.	What is the effect of adoption of a motion to table?

47.	What are the basic rules governing the motion to table?

# CHAPTER 10
## Privileged Motions

1.  What is the purpose of a "question of privilege"?

2.  How does the presiding officer handle a question of privilege?

3.  What may a member do if the member disagrees with the decision of the presiding officer not to permit a question of privilege or not to grant a request made as a question of privilege?

4.  Explain the difference between a question of privilege of the assembly and a question of personal privilege.

5.  Explain how motions may be introduced as a question of privilege, and how they are handled.

6.  What are the basic rules governing a question of privilege?

7.  What is the purpose of a motion to recess?

8.  What is the difference between recess and adjourn?

9. What are the limitations and restrictions on a motion to recess?

10. What are the basic rules governing the motion to recess?

11. What is the purpose of a motion to adjourn?

12. When is the motion to adjourn privileged, and when is it not privileged?

13. How may the motion to adjourn be debated or amended?

14. When a motion to adjourn is made and there is still important business to conduct, what should happen?

15. When an assembly cannot consider all its important business in the time available for a meeting, what motion should be made?

16. What is the difference between adjournment and dissolution?

17. Who makes the decision on whether to adjourn?

18.     When adjournment has a previously set time, who adjourns
        the meeting?



19.     What happens to business that is interrupted by adjourn-
        ment?



20.     What are the basic rules governing the motion to adjourn?

This page intentionally left blank.

# CHAPTER 11
## Incidental Motions

1.  What is the purpose of a motion to appeal?

2.  In what situations may an appeal be made?

3.  When may an appeal be made?

4.  How does the presiding officer state the question on an appeal?

5.  How does the chair handle debate on an appeal?

6.  What vote is required on an appeal?

7.  What is the effect of a motion to appeal?

8.  What are the basic rules governing the motion to appeal?

9.    What is the purpose of the motion to suspend the rules?

10.    Which rules can be suspended and which rules cannot be suspended?

11.    What are the restrictions and time limits on suspension of rules?

12.    What is the Gordian Knot motion?

13.    What is the effect of adopting a motion to suspend the rules?

14.    What are the basic rules governing the motion to suspend the rules?

15.    What is the purpose of the motion to consider informally?

16.    What is the effect of adoption of a motion to consider informally?

17. What are the basic rules governing the motion to consider informally?

18. What is the purpose of point of order?

19. When may a point of order be raised?

20. How does the presiding officer respond to a point of order?

21. .What are the basic rules governing the point of order?

22. What is the purpose of an inquiry? What kind of inquiries are there?

23. To whom is the inquiry addressed?

24. May inquiries interrupt a speaker, and if so, what is the effect of interruption?

25. What are the basic rules governing inquiries?

26.    What is the purpose of a request to withdraw a motion?

27.    When can a motion be withdrawn?

28.    How is the motion to withdraw recorded in the minutes?

29.    What are the basic rules governing the request to withdraw a motion?

30.    What is the purpose of a request for a division of a question?

31.    When are motions divided by the presiding officer, and when are they divided by the assembly?

32.    What is the purpose of a request to consider a motion by paragraph?

33.    When may a division of a question be proposed?

34. What are the basic rules governing the request for a division of a question or for consideration by paragraph?


35. What is the purpose of the call for a division of the assembly?


36. When may a division of the assembly be requested?


37. What are the basic rules governing the call for a division of the assembly?

This page intentionally left blank.

# CHAPTER 12
## Types of Meetings

1. Define a meeting.

2. Define a convention.

3. What is a regular meeting?

4. What is a special meeting?

5. When are minutes of a special meeting read?

6. How is a continued meeting defined?

7. Under what type of meeting do boards and committees operate?

8. List some rules to be used when some members are grouped together in one location with others participating at individual locations.

9. List some basic rules that must be established for meetings in which members are not in the same place.

# CHAPTER 13
## Notice of Meetings and Proposals

1.  Why is notice important?

2.  What should a notice of meeting contain?

3.  How are convention notices most often issued?

4.  What should notice of a special meeting contain?

5.  Do continued meetings require notice?

6.  List the two ways a member may waive notice?

7.  In a proposal that is required by law, charter, or by a provision in the bylaws to be given notice, how should the proposal be stated in the call to the meeting?

8.  If the organization's bylaws set the number of members of the board at 13 and notice was given to reduce the number to 9 members, what amendments to the proposal would be permitted?

This page intentionally left blank.

# CHAPTER 14
## Order of Business and Agenda

1.  What is an order of business?

2.  What is the common parliamentary law pattern for an order of business?

3.  Where is a prayer, opening ceremony, or roll call included in an order of business?

4.  What is the order of business for a special meeting?

5.  What is the order of business for a convention?

6.  What is an agenda?

7.  How is the postponement of reading of the minutes handled?

8.  What action is taken on the treasurer's report?

9.    What does unfinished business contain?

10.   What does new business contain?

11.   Why should "announcements" be part of the order of business?

12.   Who adjourns the meeting?

13.   In a convention, when a program has been adopted and a time fixed for considering certain items of business, how may the schedule of business items be deviated from?

14.   What is a consent agenda?

15.   What is the procedure for removing an item from the consent agenda for separate consideration?

16.   How is a consent agenda established?"

17.   What is a priority agenda?

# CHAPTER 15
## Quorum

1.   Define a quorum.



2.   What is the quorum requirement for a regular meeting, a mass meeting, a convention, boards and committees?



3.   What does a quorum refer to?



4.   In computing a quorum, who is counted?



5.   Does a member with a personal interest in a question affect the quorum?



6.   What does the term "in good standing" mean?



7.   Whose duty is it to raise a question on quorum?



8.   How is the presence of a quorum determined?

9.    When is a quorum presumed to be present?

# CHAPTER 16
## Debate

1. How is debate regulated?


2. What is the extent of debate on motions?


3. What motions are fully debatable?


4. What motions are debatable with restrictions?


5. What motions are not debatable?


6. How does a member obtain the floor?


7. When several seek recognition at the same time, how does the presiding officer decide which member should be recognized?


8. When may a person speak more than once?


9. What is NOT debate?

10.    How is relevancy in debate determined?




11.    What is meant by "dilatory tactics"?




12.    How should a member conduct himself during debate?




13.    What are the presiding officer's duties during debate?




14.    What are the time limits on debate?




15.    How is a question brought to a vote?




16.    How is informal consideration brought about?




17.    How is informal consideration terminated?

# CHAPTER 17
## Votes Required for Valid Action

1. What is the significance of a majority vote?

2. What is the meaning of "majority vote" as it is used in *AIPSC*?

3. Under what circumstances may a proposal or an election be decided other than by majority vote?

4. What happens when more than a majority vote is required?

5. What is an exception to the principle of requiring only a majority vote?

6. Where should vote requirements be defined?

7. List various ways that a majority vote can be computed.

8. What is meant by "a majority vote of all the members in good standing"?

9.  The bylaws state that a certain class of motions must be adopted by at least a majority of the quorum. The quorum is 100 members. What is the minimum number of members required to vote in the affirmative to adopt a motion in this class of motions?

10. Why are abstentions not counted?

11. What is a plurality vote?

12. When can a candidate be elected by plurality vote?

13. What is unanimous vote?

14. What is a tie vote?

15. When does the presiding officer vote?

16. What is a simple formula for computing a two-thirds vote?

17. When officers of equal rank are being voted on simultaneously and require a majority vote, what are the requirements for election?

18.    What is meant by a double majority?


19.    When can a member NOT vote?

This page intentionally left blank.

# CHAPTER 18
## Methods of Voting

1. What is a vote?

2. What are the usual methods of voting?

3. What is general consent and when is it appropriate to use this voting method?

4. If the presiding officer tries to take a vote by general consent and a member wishes to take a vote, what should the member say?

5. If a member believes a vote is indecisive, what should the member do?

6. If a motion appears to be adopted unanimously, may the presiding officer dispense with taking the negative vote? Is there an exception?

7. Explain how a roll call vote is taken.

8.    When can an organization use voting by mail?

9.    What are the advantages and disadvantages of voting by mail?

10.   What is the advantage of electronic voting?

11.   What is a proxy?

12.   Can proxies be used to establish a quorum?

13.   Describe *AIPSC*'s default preferential voting system.

14.   What is the Borda Count method of voting?

15.   When may a member change his vote?

16.   What is a straw vote? Is it a binding vote if taken during a meeting? Why?

# CHAPTER 19
## Nominations and Elections

1. What should the bylaw provisions on nominations contain?

2. What should the bylaw provision on elections contain?

3. What is a nomination?

4. Are nominations from the floor permitted?

5. Is relying solely on nominations from the floor a good method?

6. How are nominations from the floor closed?

7. By what means may a member, who was not nominated by a committee or from the floor, be elected?

8. What are some reasons for the selection of a nominating committee?

9.  How is a nominating committee selected?

10. Which member of the board should NOT be on the nominating committee?

11. What are the duties usually assigned to a nominating committee?

12. Where are the qualifications of nominees listed?

13. Can a member become a candidate for another office without giving up his or her currently held office?

14. May members of the nominating committee become candidates?

15. Should an organization require a multiple slate of nominees?

16. Who should serve on an election committee?

17. Who has a right to observe the counting of ballots?

18.   List some rules governing the legality of ballots.

19.   Give the requirements of a report of an election committee.

20.   What vote is necessary to elect?

21.   When does an election become effective?

22.   When may an election be challenged?

This page intentionally left blank.

# CHAPTER 20
## Officers

1. *American Institute of Parliamentarians Standard Code of Parliamentary Procedure (AIPSC)* states that the president or the head of an organization, whatever the title may be, has three roles. What are they?

2. What are the fundamental qualities of the president as a leader?

3. List some important duties usually performed by the president as administrator.

4. A member moves to adjourn before some important business is conducted. What should the presiding officer do?

5. What are the duties of the president as presiding officer?

6. What are the duties of the president-elect?

7. What are the duties of the vice president?

8. What are the chief duties of the secretary?

9. May an elected secretary propose a motion in a meeting while acting as secretary to the meeting?

10. What are the duties of the corresponding secretary?

11. What are the duties of the treasurer?

12. What are the duties of the member parliamentarian?

13. What are the duties of the sergeant-at-arms?

14. The bylaws restrict officers from serving more than one term in the same office. The president resigned and the vice president became president to complete the term. Is the new president restricted from being elected president in his own right?

15. How are vacancies filled?

16.    How is an officer or director removed from office?


17.    What are the common valid causes for removal from office?


18.    What conduct of an officer is NOT a valid reason for removal from office?

This page intentionally left blank.

# CHAPTER 21
## Committees and Boards

1.   Why are committees important?

2.   What are the advantages of committees?

3.   What is a standing committee?

4.   Where are the specifics of the standing committee found?

5.   What is a special committee sometimes called?

6.   How are special committees classified?

7.   If no committee chair is elected or appointed, how does the committee obtain a chair?

8.   How are standing committee members selected?

9. What are the rights of an ex officio member?

10. Should the president be an ex officio member of all committees?

11. Where are the powers, rights, and duties of a special committee found?

12. Under whose control are all committees?

13. How may a committee member be replaced?

14. Can a committee represent the organization to an outside person or organization?

15. What information should the secretary furnish to each committee?

16. Who may attend committee meetings?

17.    What is the procedure in a committee meeting?

18.    What is a committee hearing?

19.    What is a governing board?

20.    Who generally composes the governing board of an organization?

21.    Where are the duties, responsibilities, and powers of the board of directors defined?

22.    What authority do members of a governing board have?

23.    How does an executive committee come into being?

24.    Is it necessary to have a conflict of interest policy?

This page intentionally left blank.

# CHAPTER 22
## Committee Reports and Recommendations

1.  What do committee reports usually include?

2.  Is the report of a committee valid if made without a meeting? Why?

3.  How is a committee report presented?

4.  May a report be amended at the meeting when it is presented to the assembly?

5.  How is a committee report disposed of?

6.  Is a committee report included in the minutes?

7.  What should be recorded in the minutes concerning a committee report?

8.  When can a minority report be presented?

9. When may committee recommendations be presented?

10. How should a committee recommendation be stated?

# CHAPTER 23
## Conventions and Their Committees

1. What is a convention?

2. Should voting delegates be instructed on how to vote? Why?

3. What is the responsibility of a delegate?

4. What are the duties of an alternate delegate?

5. What are the committees common to most conventions?

6. What is the order in which these committees report?

7. When is the official list of delegates to a convention established?

8. What does the credentials committee report contain?

9. What does the rules committee report contain?

10. What vote is required to adopt the convention rules?

11. What vote is required to suspend a convention standing rule?

12. Who gives permission to make subsequent changes to the agenda once it is adopted?

13. What are the duties of the teller's committee?

14. What is a bylaws or governance committee often empowered to do?

15. What limitation should be imposed on a bylaws or governance committee?

# CHAPTER 24
## Reference (or Resolutions) Committees

1. What is the purpose of a reference committee?

2. What is the composition of reference committee members?

3. Who appoints the reference committee members?

4. What are the advantages of a reference committee system?

5. In organizations with large conventions, how are proposals for considerations submitted?

6. Who presides at the hearing of a reference committee?

7. During the hearing, what restrictions, if any, are imposed at the hearing?

8. During the hearing, can motions to amend a resolution be made?

9. In a reference committee hearing, may a member of the reference committee express opinions during the hearing?

10. After a hearing, what does the reference committee do?

11. How is the report of the reference committee given?

12. What requirements are necessary regarding the wording of reference committee recommendations?

13. What is a consent agenda and how is it used in a convention?

14. When should a priority agenda be utilized?

15. What is the purpose of the motion to adopt in-lieu-of?

16. What is the process for using the motion to adopt in-lieu-of?

17. What happens when the adopt in-lieu-of motion is defeated?

18.    Does the reference committee take the place of a vigilant and
       knowledgeable membership?

This page intentionally left blank.

# CHAPTER 25
## Minutes

1.  What is the importance of minutes?

2.  What are the responsibilities of the secretary?

3.  Who can inspect the minutes?

4.  What is the appropriate format that minutes must use?

5.  When should the minutes be prepared?

6.  Can any member request to see the minutes of a closed meeting (executive session)?

7.  Are minutes kept in a committee meeting and if so, for what purpose?

8.  What should minutes contain?

9.   What should minutes NOT contain?

10.   How are corrections made to the minutes?

11.   When may minutes be corrected?

12.   When should a minutes approving committee be used?

13.   What are the various forms of published minutes?

14.   What must be considered to ensure proper retention of the electronic minutes?

15.   Can the minutes be approved as distributed with the motion to "dispense with the reading of the minutes"?

16.   What are the shortcuts that a secretary may use for taking minutes during a meeting?

17.   What is the general purpose of an action log?

# CHAPTER 26
## Governing Documents: Charters, Bylaws, and Rules

1. What are the types of governing documents of an organization?

2. What are the two types of charters?

3. Who approves amendment of a charter granted by the government?

4. If the constitution and bylaws are two separate documents, what should each address?

5. What is the function of bylaws?

6. When drafting the bylaws, what level of detail is needed?

7. What vote is required to adopt original bylaws?

8. When do bylaws go into effect?

9.  What specific requirements should be in the bylaws concerning amending bylaws?

10. What is a simple method of stating a proposed amendment?

11. How are bylaws amendments considered?

12. What vote is required on amendments to bylaws?

13. What is a revision of bylaws?

14. What vote is required to adopt a revision to the bylaws?

15. Who has the final say on the interpretation of bylaws?

16. What are standing rules?

17. How might an organization cite the *American Institute of Parliamentarians Standard Code of Parliamentary Procedure* in its bylaws as the organization's parliamentary authority?

18.	Where should detailed procedures be placed?




19.	Bylaws define the structure of an organization. What do policies define?




20.	If a proposal is contrary to an adopted policy of the organization, how should the presiding officer deal with it?

This page intentionally left blank.

# CHAPTER 27
## Finances

1.  What are some considerations needed when developing an accounting system?

2.  What should the treasurer's report contain?

3.  How is the treasurer's report dealt or disposed with?

4.  What are the usual duties of a finance committee?

5.  Who selects the auditor?

6.  Which profession is authorized by law to express professional and independent opinions on the financial statements of an organization?

7.  The auditor's report is an opinion on the treasurer's report. What are the two types of report that the auditors provide?

8.  What are some financial safeguards that an organization can adopt?




9.  What is a budget?




10. Who should approve unusual or particular large expenditures?

# CHAPTER 28
## Types of Organizations

1.  What is the difference between a temporary and a permanent organization?

2.  What are some of the common forms of nonprofit and business entities?

3.  Unincorporated nonprofit entities that are rather loosely structured and operate only under a set of their own governing documents are termed _____ _____.

4.  What are the chief advantages of incorporation?

5.  What are the statutory requirements if a nonprofit association is incorporated?

6.  What is the main requirement of a nonprofit corporation?

7.  If a nonprofit organization receives profit incidental to its operation, how must that profit be used?

8.  May an unincorporated nonprofit organization qualify as a tax-exempt entity?

# CHAPTER 29
## Rights of Members and of Organizations

1.  What is the relationship between a member and the organization?

2.  What are the fundamental rights of members?

3.  What is the definition of a member in good standing?

4.  List some of the fundamental rights of an organization.

5.  How should the individual member regard his rights in relation to the rights of other members and of the organization?

6.  How do the rights of others and of the organization surpass the rights of the individual?

7.  Procedures for the discipline and expulsion of members should be included _____ _____ _____ _____.

8. When is termination of membership justified?

9. What are the essential steps for imposing severe discipline or expelling a member?

10. When does a member have the right to resign?

11. When does a resignation become effective?

12. Can an officer or director who has resigned either orally or in writing resume office because of a change of mind?

# CHAPTER 30
## Staff and Consultants

1.   To whom is the executive director responsible?

2.   What other professional individuals may an organization find advantageous to hire?

3.   What are the situations in which an attorney's services are essential?

4.   What are the duties of the parliamentarian?

5.   Under whose direction does the parliamentarian usually work?

6.   Where does the parliamentarian usually sit during a convention?

7.   Under what circumstances might a parliamentarian preside?

This page intentionally left blank.

# SECTION 2
# ANSWERS TO
# CONCEPTS AND RULES IN *AIPSC*

This page intentionally left blank.

# CHAPTER 1
## Parliamentary Law

1. What are two main historical purposes of "the rules of proceeding"?

   The rules operate as a check and control on the actions of the majority, and as a shelter and protection to the minority against the attempts of power. **p. 1**.

2. Name some of the procedural safeguards found in law.

   Some of the procedural safeguards found in law are the right to be informed, the right to attend hearings and meetings, the right to speak out, the right to due process, the right to complain when process is not followed, and the right to take civil action. **p. 2**.

3. What are the procedures available to members to complain when procedure is not followed in a meeting, and to further complain when they believe the presiding officer is unfair or incorrect?

   Members may raise a point of order, and may use an appeal to pursue the matter further. **p. 2.**

4. What are some of the underlying principles for the rules of debate?

   The rules are to assure that debate is orderly, courteous, fair, and usually available to all members. **p. 2.**

5. What is the purpose of meeting procedures?

   The purpose of meeting procedures is to allow members to reach informed business decisions in an effective, efficient, orderly, courteous, and fair manner. They facilitate group decisions and allow the members to work as a cohesive group, and to reach decisions through debate and majority vote. **p. 2.**

6.   Where can meeting procedures be found?

Meeting procedures can be found in statutes (federal, state, or local), regulations, the charter of a parent organization, bylaws, adopted standing and special rules, and in an adopted parliamentary authority. Other procedural rules may derive from the common law of parliamentary procedure, itself derived from judicial decisions and custom. **p. 3**.

7.   What is the relationship of customary procedure and written rules of procedure?

Some rules may be customary, based on usage, but written rules have precedence over custom when brought to the attention of the meeting. **p. 3.**

8.   What rules constitute "parliamentary law"?

All of the rules in statutes, regulations, charters, bylaws, adopted rules, adopted parliamentary authority, and custom, as well as in common law, taken together, constitute parliamentary law. **p. 3.**

9.   Give one or more examples of an abuse of parliamentary law,

Use of parliamentary law for personal gain, or to harm the organization, or to thwart the will of the assembly, or for no other reason but to delay the meeting, are examples of abuse of parliamentary law. **pp. 3-4.**

10.   What should be done about tactics that abuse the use of parliamentary law?

Tactics that abuse the use of parliamentary law should not be tolerated by the presiding officer or the other attendees of the meeting. **p. 4.**

11.   Name several kinds of organizations that use parliamentary law.

Parliamentary law is used by governmental bodies, associations, boards, commissions, and labor unions. **p. 4.**

12.  Why might the meetings of organizations be required to use parliamentary law?

Parliamentary law might be imposed on an organization by statute, common law, or by a superior body, but often it is deliberately chosen. **p 4.**

13.  What is the difference in procedure between large organizations and small organizations?

Procedure is often more formal and more rigidly applied in large meetings, while in smaller meetings, formal procedure may be minimal, but must still conform to the fundamental principles in the parliamentary authority. **p. 4.**

14.  What is a parliamentary authority?

A parliamentary authority is a written set of principles and specific procedural rules that determines the rules to be followed in all meetings of the organization, unless superseded by other rules adopted by the organization. **p. 5.**

15.  What are the rules called that are adopted by the organization to supersede the parliamentary authority?

They may be called special rules or standing rules. **p. 5**.

16.  Why might an organization choose to adopt special rules to supersede the parliamentary authority?

Organizations might choose to adopt special rules to supersede the parliamentary authority in order to meet the specific needs of that organization. **p. 5.**

This page intentionally left blank.

# CHAPTER 2
## Fundamental Principles of Parliamentary Law

1.    What is the purpose of parliamentary law?

The purpose of parliamentary law is to facilitate the orderly transaction of business and to promote cooperation and harmony. The philosophy of parliamentary law is to be constructive. Parliamentary law makes it easier for people to work together effectively and is designed to help organizations and members to accomplish their purposes. **p. 7.**

2.    For what purposes should parliamentary procedure NOT be used?

Parliamentary law should not be used to awe, entangle, or confuse the uninitiated. **p. 7.**

3.    What are two of the basic procedural rules that assure the simplest and most direct procedure for accomplishing a purpose?

Two of the basic procedural rules are: first, the order of precedence of motions; and second, only one motion may be considered at a time. **p. 7.**

4.    What are the fundamental rights of all people and all members?

All people have a fundamental right of association and of assembly. **p. 7.**

Members have equal rights to propose motions, speak, ask questions, nominate, be a candidate for office, vote, or exercise any other privilege of a member. **p. 8.**

5.    What should the presiding officer do in regard to equality of the members' rights?

The presiding officer should be strictly impartial and should act promptly to protect the equality of all members in the exercise of their rights and privileges. **p. 8.**

6.  What is the ultimate authority of an organization vested in?

    The ultimate authority of an organization is, as a general matter, vested in a majority of its members. **p. 8.**

7.  By joining an organization, a member agrees to be governed by the vote of its majority. **p. 8.**

8.  What are the rights of members?

    -   When in the minority, to be protected and to have the same consideration and respect as members who are in the majority.
    -   The right to present proposals, be heard, and to oppose proposals.
    -   The right of full and free discussion of every proposition presented for decision.
    -   The right to know the meaning of the question before the assembly and what its effect will be.
    -   That all meetings be characterized by fairness and good faith. **pp. 9-10.**

9.  John Hatsell in 1776 wrote, "Motives ought to outweigh objections of form." What did he mean?

    The intent and overall good faith of the group are more important than the particular detail of procedure used in a given instance. **p. 10.**

# CHAPTER 3
## Classification of Motions

1.  How are motions classified into groups?

    Motions are classified into five groups: main motions, specific main motions, subsidiary motions, privileged motions, and incidental motions. **p. 11.**

2.  What is the purpose of a main motion?

    The purpose of a main motion is to bring substantive proposal before the assembly for consideration and action. **p. 11.**

3.  What are the six main motions that have specific names and are governed by somewhat different rules?

    These six main motions are called specific main motions because they perform unique and specific functions. They do not present a new proposal, but they concern actions that were previously taken. The specific main motions are: adopt in-lieu-of, amend a previous action, ratify, recall from a committee (or board), reconsider, and rescind. **p. 11.**

4.  Define subsidiary motions.

    Subsidiary motions alter the main motion, or delay or hasten its consideration. Subsidiary motions are usually applied to main motions, but some of them may be applied to certain other motions. **p. 12.**

5.  What are the most frequently used subsidiary motions?

    The most frequently used subsidiary motions are: (from highest to lowest in rank): table, close debate and vote immediately, limit or extend debate, postpone to a certain time, refer to a committee, and amend. **p. 12.**

6.    Define privileged motions.

Privileged motions are emergency motions of such urgency that they are entitled to immediate consideration. They relate to the members, to the organization, and to the meeting as whole rather than to particular items of business. **p. 12.**

7.    Name the privileged motions.

There are three privileged motions (from highest to lowest iin rank): adjourn, recess, and question of privilege. **p. 12.**

8.    Define incidental motions.

Incidental motions arise incidentally out of the business before the assembly. They do not relate directly to the main motion or to specific main motions, but usually relate to matters incidental to the conduct of the meeting. **p. 12.**

9.    Name the incidental motions.

The incidental motions include: appeal from a decision of the chair, suspend the rules, consider informally, point of order, inquiry, withdrawal of a motion, division of a question, and division of the assembly. **p. 13.**

10.    What other motions may be made?

There are other unlisted motions that members may make. For example a member may move that a vote be taken by roll call. Since this motion clearly arises incidentally out of the business before the assembly, it is an incidental motion. A member might move that an article related to the business under consideration be read to the assembly before voting occurs; this would be a privileged motion due to its urgency. **p. 13.**

11. What subsidiary, privileged, and incidental motions may be main motions if proposed when no main motion is pending?

The following subsidiary, privileged and incidental motions may be made as main motions when no other business is pending: limit debate, postpone to a certain time, and refer to a committee may be stated as main motions. All privileged motions may be stated as main motions. Appeal from the decision of the chair and suspend the rules, which are normally stated as incidental motions, may be stated as main motions. **pp. 14-15.**

12. Name at least two features of incidental motions.

Incidental motions may be offered at any time, have no order of rank and are disposed of prior to the business out of which they arise. **p. 12.**

13. Because of their nature some incidental motions have two other distinguishing features. Name them.

Some incidental motions may interrupt business and in some cases may interrupt a speaker. **p. 12.**

14. A main motion is pending and a member moves, "that we take the vote by roll call." What type of motion is this?

Although not listed in the classification of motions in *American Institute of Parliamentarians Standard Code*, it is clearly incidental to the pending main motion. Because this motion arises incidentally out of the business before the assembly, it is an incidental motion. **p. 13.**

15. A member moves to table the pending main motion until 3 p.m. How should the presiding officer handle such a motion?

The presiding officer should recognize that the member wishes to postpone the pending business to 3 p.m. and not to table it. The presiding officer after querying the member should state the motion as intended by the mover, in this case, likely as a motion to postpone. **p. 13.**

16. If a subsidiary or privileged motion is stated when no other motions are pending, what classification is the motion?

It is a main motion and retains the same governing rules as a main motion. **p. 14.**

# CHAPTER 4
## Ranking of Motions

1.   What does the rank or precedence of a motion determine?

     The rank of a motion determines its priority when it is proposed, and the sequence in which it must considered, and disposed of. The purpose of the rank of a motion is to ensure that each motion is dealt with consistently and without confusion. **p. 16.**

2.   Name the privileged motions from the highest to the lowest ranking in order of precedence.

     In order of rank the privileged motions are, from the highest: adjourn, recess, and question of privilege. **p. 16.**

3.   Name the subsidiary motions from the highest to the lowest ranking in order of precedence.

     In order of rank the subsidiary motions are, from the highest: table, close debate, limit or extend debate, postpone to a certain time, refer to a committee, and amend. **p. 16.**

4.   What rank do incidental motions have?

     Incidental motions have no order of ranking. They can arise incidentally out of the immediately pending business at any time, and they must be decided as soon as they arise. **p. 17.**

5.   What are the two basic rules of ranking?

     The two basic rules of ranking are:

     •   When a motion is being considered, any motion of higher rank may be proposed, but no motion of lower rank may be proposed.

     •   Motions are considered and voted on in reverse order of their proposal. The motion last proposed, and which is the highest ranked motion pending, is considered and disposed of first. **pp. 16-17.**

6. A main motion has been moved, followed by a motion to refer to a committee. A member wishes to amend the main motion. Would this be permitted?

   No, it would not be permitted. The motion to amend, in the current parliamentary situation, could be applied to only the motion to refer. After the motion to refer has been disposed of, and if the main motion is then pending, a motion to amend could be applied to the main motion. **pp. 17-18, inside front cover**.

7. A main motion is moved, followed by a motion to table. What motions would now be in order?

   Only the privileged motions and some incidental motions may be made at this time. **pp. 17-18, inside front cover.**

8. A main motion, the motion to amend, the motion to limit debate, and the motion to recess are pending. Which motions would now be in order?

   The privileged motion to adjourn would be in order and any incidental motion arising out of the parliamentary situation would be in order. Because the motion to recess is amendable, it would also be in order to move a motion to amend the motion to recess. **pp. 17-18, inside front cover.**

9. Define a pending motion or question.

   A pending motion or question is one which has been proposed and stated to the assembly by the presiding officer, but not yet decided. **p. 18**.

10. What is meant by the immediately pending motion or question?

    The immediately pending motion or question is the particular motion being considered by the assembly at any particular time. **p. 18.**

# CHAPTER 5
## Rules Governing Motions

1.   What are the nine rules you need to know about each motion?

For each motion you need to know the following nine rules: can the motion interrupt a speaker, does the motion require a second, is the motion debatable, can the motion be amended, what vote does the motion require, what is the ranking of the motion, to what other motions can the motion apply, what other motions can be applied to the motion, and can the motion be renewed. **p. 19.**

2.   What two types of motions can interrupt a speaker?

There are two types of motions that because of their urgency, can interrupt a speaker. The first are those that are subject to a time limit to move the motion, such as the motions to reconsider, to appeal, division of the assembly, and a request to withdraw a motion. The second are those motions that that relate to the immediate rights and privileges of a member or of the assembly: question of privilege, point of order, factual inquiry, and parliamentary inquiry. **pp. 19-20.**

3.   What motions require a second? What are the exceptions?

Motions normally require a second except in meetings of committees, boards, or some government bodies.

A few actions do not require a second, because, although classified as motions, they are *requests* that are decided, or must be granted, by the presiding officer. Those that do not require a second are point of order, factual and parliamentary inquiries, withdrawal of a motion, division of a question, division of the assembly, and question of privilege. Questions of privilege, division of a question, and withdrawal of a motion are sometimes presented as motions instead of requests, in which case they require seconds. **p. 20.**

4. Are all motions debatable?

Not all motions are debatable. Some are open to full debate, others are open to restricted debate, and still others are undebatable. **p. 21, inside front cover**.

5. Can all motions be amended?

Not all motions are amendable. A motion can be amended if it contains wording that can be varied, as long as the change in wording does not change the motion into a different kind of motion. Some motions can be amended freely while some motions can be amended only within restrictions. **p. 22, inside front cover.**

6. What vote do motions require?

Most motions require a majority vote to adopt. Motions that affect the rights of members may require a two-thirds vote. These motions limit the rights of members to propose, discuss, and decide proposals and include motions to amend to close debate, limit debate, table, and suspend the rules. An organization's bylaws may provide that certain other motions require a two-thirds vote. For example, most bylaws require a two-thirds vote to amend the bylaws, and in some states statutory law requires a two-thirds vote for a nonprofit membership corporation to buy, sell, or lease real estate or to mortgage substantially of of its property. **pp. 22-23**.

7. Explain the ranking (precedence) of motions.

The ranking of motions determines the order in which they may be proposed, and in which they must be disposed of. When a motion is before the assembly, any motion is in order if it has a higher rank (order of precedence) than the immediately pending motion, but no motion having a lower rank is in order. Motions are considered and decided in reverse order to that of their proposal. Incidental motions have no order of rank, may be proposed when needed, and are decided upon immediately. **p. 23**.

8. To what other motions can motions apply?

A motion is said to apply to another motion when it is used to alter or dispose of or affect the original motion in some way. For example, the motion to amend applies to all amendable motions; the motions to close debate and to debate apply to all debatable motions; the motion to withdraw applies to any motion; and division of the question applies to main motions. There are many other examples of motions applying to other motions. **pp. 23-24, inside front cover.**

9. Can a motion be renewed?

As a general rule, when a main motion has been voted on and has lost, the same, or substantially the same, motion cannot be proposed again at the same meeting or convention, but it may be reconsidered. Use of the motion to reconsider is required to bring such a substantive main motion before the assembly again.

A main motion that was rejected at a previous meeting may be renewed at any subsequent meeting, but a main motion that was adopted at a previous meeting may only be considered again by use of the specific main motions to rescind (repeal), or to amend the previously adopted action. Motions that are procedural rather than substantive may be renewed at the discretion of the presiding officer, based on the likelihood of a different outcome if the motion is considered again. For example, a defeated motion to refer may be renewed if the main motion has been amended and now presents a somewhat different question, or if (after a passage of time) the defeated procedural motion appears now to have merit in spite of the assembly's earlier decision to defeat it. **pp. 24-25.**

10. What is repeal by implication?

Repeal by implication automatically results from the adoption of a motion that conflicts in whole or in part with another motion or motions previously adopted. The first motion is repealed only to the extent that its provisions cannot be reconciled with those of the new motion. Repeal by implication is intended to correct *inadvertent* conflicts, not to be a blanket method of disposing of previously adopted main motions without voting directly on their repeal. **pp. 25-26**.

# CHAPTER 6
## Processing of Motions

1.    What is a motion?

      A motion is a formal statement of a proposal or question to an assembly to take action or express certain sentiments. **p. 27.**

2.    What are the steps in presenting a motion?

      There are five steps usually required in presenting a motion: the member rises and addresses the presiding officer, the member is recognized by the presiding officer, the member proposes a motion, another member seconds the motion, and the presiding officer states the motion to the assembly. **p. 27.**

3.    When a member addresses the presiding officer, what does it indicate?

      It indicates that the member wishes to obtain the floor, that is, to have the right to present a motion or to speak. **p. 27.**

4.    How is the presiding officer addressed?

      The member rises and addresses the presiding officer by his or her official title. If the member does not know the appropriate or official title the member should address the presiding officer as "Madam Chair" or "Mister Chair." These last two titles are always correct. In large assemblies with a microphone system, members form a line at the appropriate microphone and the presiding officer recognizes members based on the microphone number or location. **pp. 27-28.**

5.    How does the presiding officer recognize a member?

The presiding officer should recognize all members in the same manner to avoid the perception of favoritism. For instance, if the presiding officer does not know every member by name, another form of recognition must be used, such as "The speaker at microphone A" or "The member in row 4." **p. 28.**

6. When a member seeking the floor does not obtain it, what does the member do?

The member who was seeking recognition should be seated as soon as one member is recognized. If a microphone system is being used, members in line may keep their places in line, but they should step back to avoid crowding the member who has the floor. **p. 28.**

7. How must a motion be proposed?

A motion should be stated in the form, "I move that ...," followed by a statement of the proposal that the member wishes to bring before the assembly. **p. 28.**

8. If a member says, "Madam President, I suggest that ...," what should the presiding officer say?

The presiding officer may recognize this as debate, or may inquire whether the member wishes to put the statement in the form of a motion. **p. 28.**

9. If a member has a lengthy, complicated, or important motion, how should the member submit the motion?

A lengthy, complicated, or important motion should be submitted in writing to the presiding officer and the secretary. **p. 29.**

10. What does a second indicate?

Seconding a motion merely indicates that the member wishes the motion to be considered by the assembly; it is not necessarily an endorsement of the motion. **p. 29.**

11.    If there is no second what does the presiding officer say?

       If the motion is not seconded, the presiding officer asks, "Is there a second to this motion?" If the meaning of the motion is not clear to the members, the presiding officer should ask the proposing member to state the motion more clearly, and then ask again if there is a second. If there is no second, the presiding officer may say, "There is no second. The motion is not before the assembly," and proceed to other business. **p. 29.**

12.    If a member objects to the lack of a second, what does the presiding officer do?

       If any member objects to the lack of a second, the presiding officer must call for one, unless debate by more than one member has already occurred, fulfilling the purpose of a second (indication that more than one member wishes the motion to be considered). **p. 29.**

13.    Name two situations where a second is not required.

       A second is not required for a motion submitted to the superior body by a committee. It is also not required for motions made in a committee or a small board. **p. 30.**

14.    Which is the legal motion, the one stated by the chair or the one stated by a member?

       If there is a difference of opinion as to what the exact wording of a motion should be, the motion as stated by the member is the legal motion. **p. 30.**

15.    When a motion has been properly moved and seconded, what does the presiding officer say?

       The presiding officer states the motion to the assembly as correctly and clearly as possible by saying, "It has been moved and seconded that ...." In a large assembly, it is useful to have motions in writing and projected on a screen, in which case the presiding officer, after confirming that the written motion is correct, may dispense with stating the entire motion (by requesting permission of the assembly to do so) and directing the assembly to the written version. **p. 30.**

16. When is a motion called a 'pending question' or a 'pending motion'?

From the time a motion is stated by the presiding officer until it is disposed of, it is called a "pending question" or "pending motion." **p. 30.**

17. What are the seven steps in voting on a motion?

The presiding officer (1) restates the pending question, (2) takes the affirmative vote, (3) takes the negative vote, (4) announces which side prevailed, (5) announces whether the motion was adopted or defeated, (6) announces what will be done as a result of the vote, and (7) introduces the next item of business or calls for further business. **pp. 31-32.**

18. Why does the presiding officer restate the pending motion before any other steps in voting?

The presiding officer restates the pending motion before any other steps in voting to assure that the members know what they are voting on and know the effect of adoption or defeat of the motion. **p. 32.**

19. How are the affirmative and negative votes taken?

For a voice vote, the presiding officer says "All in favor, say aye" and then "All opposed, say no". For a vote by division or for a two-thirds vote, the presiding officer says "All in favor, rise. Be seated" and "All opposed, rise. Be seated." In small groups, the presiding officer may instruct members to raise their hands to indicate their preference. It is critical to take the affirmative and negative votes in a parallel manner, to avoid any perception that the presiding officer has any preference as to how members should vote, and to avoid language that might discourage members to vote as they wish.

**p. 32.**

20.    Should the presiding officer always take the negative vote, even if it appears that the affirmative vote is unanimous?

Yes, the presiding officer should always take the negative vote. The only exception to this is when voting on motions to honor or thank someone when it is not unusual for the assembly to demonstrate its approval by applause. **p. 32**.

21.    What should the presiding officer do if uncertain of which side prevailed in any vote?

If the presiding officer is uncertain of which side prevailed in a vote, the vote should be repeated using a more definitive method. If a voice vote is uncertain, a division may be attempted. If a division is uncertain, a counted vote may be needed. **p. 33.**

22.    May some or all of the steps in processing a motion be skipped or combined?

Ordinarily all the steps should be followed, but in some cases, some of the steps may not be applicable (such as recognition when the rules governing a motion allow a member to interrupt) and with routine matters, many of the steps in processing a motion can be combined or even skipped altogether. **p. 34.**

This page intentionally left blank.

# CHAPTER 7
# Main Motions

1.    What is a main motion?

      A main motion is a substantive proposal presented to the assembly for consideration, discussion, decision, and action. **p. 35.**

2.    How should a main motion be phrased?

      A main motion must be introduced by the words, "I move" Otherwise, wide latitude in wording is permitted. A motion should be concise and clear. **p. 36.**

3.    What types of main motions are usually in resolution form?

      Motions that express sentiments, or are a formal statement of the opinion of the assembly, or are highly important, or are long and involved are usually presented in the form of a resolution. **p. 36.**

4.    What is the form of a resolution?

      A resolution is usually in the form:
      I move the adoption of the following resolution: "Resolved, that..."

      Resolutions may have several resolved clauses, and may begin with one or more (optional) "Whereas" clauses, giving the background to or the reasons for the resolution. **pp. 36-37.**

5.    When may discussion of a motion or resolution begin?

      A motion may is open for debate as soon as it has been formally stated to the assembly by the presiding officer. **p. 37.**

6. What are some of the ways in which disposition of a main motion may occur?

A main motion may be decided by a vote approving or defeating the motion, or it may be disposed of by some other motion such as a motion to refer. Definite action of some kind must be taken on a main motion. **p. 37.**

7. May another main motion on the same subject be proposed while a main motion is pending?

A main motion on the same subject as the pending main motion may be offered only as an amendment by substitution. **p. 37.**

8. Discuss how a main motion may or may not be renewed when adopted or defeated.

When a main motion has been acted on and defeated, it cannot be renewed in the same or substantially the same wording at the same meeting or convention, but it may be reconsidered at the same meeting or convention, or it may be presented as a new main motion at a later meeting or convention.

When a main motion has been adopted, it may not be revisited at the same meeting except by the use of reconsideration, and it may not be revisited at a subsequent meeting except by the use of motions to amend a previous action or to rescind a motion. **pp. 37-38.**

9. What is the effect of adopting the main motion?

The effect of the adoption of the main motion is to commit the organization to the proposed action stated by the motion and approved by vote of the assembly. **p. 38.**

10. What are the basic rules governing the main motion?

The nine basic rules governing the main motion are: cannot interrupt a speaker; requires a second; is debatable because it presents a substantive proposal for consideration; can be amended; requires a majority vote; does not take precedence over other motions; applies to no other motion; can have applied to it all subsidiary motions and incidental motions to withdraw, to divide the question, and to be considered by paragraph; and cannot be renewed at the same meeting or convention, but can be reconsidered. **p. 38.**

This page intentionally left blank.

# CHAPTER 8
## Specific Main Motions

1.  What is the purpose of the motion to adopt in-lieu-of?

    The motion to adopt in-lieu-of is used to allow introduction of a main motion with the intent that its adoption will also dispose of one or more other main motions that are known to be coming before the assembly on the same, similar, or related topics. The opportunity to use a motion to adopt in-lieu-of usually arises in situations such as when main motions are required to be submitted in advance of a meeting. **p. 39.**

2.  What happens when a main motion proposed for adoption in lieu of one or more other main motions is adopted?

    When a main motion is proposed for adoption in lieu of one or more other main motions, and it is adopted, not only is the proposed motion adopted, but the other main motions that were named are defeated. **p. 39.**

3.  What happens when a main motion proposed for adoption in lieu of one or more other main motions is defeated?

    When a main motion is proposed for adoption in lieu of one or more other main motions, and it is defeated, the proposed motion is defeated, but any member may still introduce any of the other in-lieu-of motions that were named, for consideration and action by the assembly. **p. 40.**

4.  What are the basic rules governing a motion to adopt in-lieu-of? Which are different than the rules governing an original (substantive) main motion?

    Other than the features related to what happens when it is adopted or defeated, the specific main motion to adopt in-lieu-of has the same characteristics as any main motion, and is therefore governed by the same basic rules, which are:

cannot interrupt a speaker; requires a second; is debatable; can be amended; requires a majority vote; does not take precedence over other motions; applies to no other motion; can have applied to it all subsidiary motions, and the incidental motions to withdraw, to divide the question, and to be considered by paragraph; and cannot be renewed at the same meeting or convention, but can be reconsidered.

Because of the special circumstances in which the motion to *adopt in-lieu-of* is used, while it applies to no other motion, it would not be introduced unless there was at least one main motion on the same subject matter that was known to be coming before the assembly. **p. 40.**

5.     What is the purpose of a motion to amend a previous action?

The purpose of a motion to amend a previous action is to modify (amend) a main motion that was has already been adopted at a previous meeting or convention. **p. 40.**

6.     What previous actions can be amended?

Main motions approved at a previous meeting or convention can be amended. **p. 40.**

7.     Does the motion to amend a previous action affect actions that have already been taken as a result of the previous action?

The motion to amend a previous action, if adopted, affects the present and future only, and is not retroactive, so it does not affect actions that have already been taken as a result of the previously adopted motion. **p. 41.**

8.     What are the basic rules governing the motion to amend a previous action? Which are different than the rules governing an original (substantive) main motion?

The basic rules governing the specific main motion to amend a previous action is are: cannot interrupt a speaker; requires a second; is debatable; can be amended; requires the same vote (and notice, if any) that was required for adoption of the original motion; does not take precedence over other motions; applies to main motions previously adopted or actions taken at a previous meeting; can have applied to it all subsidiary motions, and the incidental motions to withdraw, division of the question, and consider by paragraph; and cannot be renewed at the same meeting or convention, but can be reconsidered.

The rules that are different than the rules governing an original (substantive) main motion are those regarding the vote required for adoption (which may be a majority, but might also require notice and/or a higher vote) and the rule about the motions to which *amend a previous action* applies. **p. 41.**

9.   Explain the purpose of the motion to ratify.

The purpose of a motion to ratify is to confirm and thereby validate an action that was taken in an emergency or when a quorum was not present, or to confirm the action or decision of another body. **pp. 41-42.**

10.   Why might a motion to ratify be needed?

The officers of an organization sometimes have to make emergency decisions when it is not possible to obtain the approval of the body that has the authority to take the action. A committee sometimes may have to take an action that exceeds its authority, and in a meeting that lacks a quorum, it is sometimes necessary to take action that cannot be delayed until a special meeting can be called or until the next regular meeting. Such actions should be ratified as soon as possible by the body with the authority to approve the otherwise improper action, at a meeting with a quorum present. **p. 42.**

11.   What are the basic rules governing the motion to ratify? Which are different than the rules governing an original (substantive) main motion?

The basic rules governing the specific main motion to ratify are: cannot interrupt a speaker; requires a second; is debatable; can be amended; requires a majority vote, unless the action being ratified would regularly require a higher vote; does not take precedence over other motions; applies to actions taken without proper authority or in the absence of a quorum, or to another body's actions that require ratification before taking effect; can have applied to it all subsidiary motions, and the incidental motions to withdraw and division of the question; and cannot be renewed at the same meeting or convention, but can be reconsidered.

The rules that are different than the rules governing an original (substantive) main motion are that it applies to actions taken without proper authority or in the absence of a quorum, or to another body's actions that require ratification before taking effect. While ratification itself might not be amended, the action being ratified may be amended. **pp. 42-43.**

12.   What is the purpose of the motion to recall a motion or subject from a committee (or board)?

The purpose of a motion to recall a motion or subject from a committee or board is to enable the assembly to remove the motion or subject from the control of a committee or board and to present it to the assembly for immediate consideration. **p. 43.**

13.   Why might a motion to recall be needed?

An assembly that has referred a pending motion or a subject to a committee or board may have reason to remove the motion or subject from the committee or board for consideration and action by the assembly or to refer the motion or subject to a different committee. **p. 44.**

14.   What is the effect of adopting a motion to recall?

Adopting a motion to recall places the original main motion and any adhering amendments before the assembly again or places the referred subject matter before the assembly for consideration. **p. 44.**

15. What are the rules governing the motion to recall a motion or subject from a committee (or board)? Which are different than the rules governing an original (substantive) main motion?

The basic rules governing the specific main motion to recall a motion or subject from a committee (or board) are: cannot interrupt a speaker; requires a second; debate is restricted to the reasons for recalling the motion or subject; cannot be amended; requires a majority vote; does not take precedence over other motions; applies to any main motion or subject that has been referred to a committee or board; can have applied to it the subsidiary motions to limit debate, close debate, and withdraw; and cannot be renewed at the same meeting or convention.

The rules that are different than the rules governing an original (substantive) main motion are that debate is limited, it cannot be amended, it applies only to main motions or subjects that have been referred to a committee or board, and that the only motions that can be applied to the motion to *recall* are the motions to limit debate, to close debate, and to withdraw. **p. 44.**

16. What is the purpose of the motion to reconsider?

The purpose of a motion to reconsider is to enable an assembly to set aside the vote on a main motion taken at the same meeting or convention and to consider the motion again as though no vote had been taken on it. **pp. 44-45.**

17. What votes can be reconsidered?

The vote on any main motion (and some specific main motions), whether adopted, defeated, or tabled, can be reconsidered at the same meeting or convention, except when something that cannot be undone has been done as a result of the vote. **p. 45**

18.     When can the motion to reconsider be offered? When is a decision on the motion made?

The motion to reconsider is unusual in that, unlike a general main motion, it can be offered at any time during a meeting, even when other business is being considered, although it cannot interrupt a speaker to do so. If the motion is proposed and seconded while other business is pending, its proposal is noted, and then it is set aside until the pending business is disposed of. After the pending business is disposed of, the motion to reconsider is immediately taken up and decided. If the motion is offered when no other business is pending, it is considered immediately. **p. 46**.

19.     Who can move to reconsider?

*AIPSC* permits any member to offer the motion to reconsider when it appears justified. **p. 47.**

20.     What is the effect of adopting the motion to reconsider?

Adoption of a motion to reconsider cancels a vote on a motion as completely as though it had never been taken and brings that motion before the assembly for consideration as though it had never been voted on. **p. 47.**

21.     What are the basic rules governing the motion to reconsider? Which are different than the rules governing an original (substantive) main motion?

The basic rules governing the specific main motion to reconsider are: can interrupt the proceedings, but not a speaker; requires a second; debate is restricted to the reasons for reconsideration; cannot be amended; requires a majority vote; does not take precedence over other motions; applies to votes on main motions taken at the same meeting or convention; can have applied to it the motions to close debate, limit debate, and to withdraw; and cannot be renewed at the same meeting or convention.

The rules that are different than the rules governing an original (substantive) main motion are that it can interrupt the proceedings, debate is limited, it cannot be amended, it applies only to votes on main motions taken at the same meeting or convention, and that the only motions that can be applied to the motion to *reconsider* are the motions to limit debate, to close debate, and to withdraw. **pp. 47-48.**

22. What is the purpose of the motion to rescind?

The purpose of the motion to rescind is to repeal (cancel, nullify, void) a main motion approved at a previous meeting. **p. 48.**

23. What is the form of the motion to rescind?

The form of the motion to rescind is, "I move to rescind the motion (state accurately and specifically the motion that is to be rescinded)." **p. 48.**

24. What motions may be rescinded?

Any main motion that was adopted, no matter how long before, may be rescinded, but the rescission does not include action taken before adoption of the motion to rescind. The motion to rescind, if adopted, affects the present and future only, since it is not retroactive. **p 48.**

25. If a member believes the motion to be rescinded might be kept with some changes, can the motion to be rescinded be amended instead?

The motion to be rescinded can be amended instead, but not while the motion to rescind is pending. While the motion to rescind is pending, a member can state the intent, as an alternative to rescinding, to offer a motion to amend the previous action if the motion to rescind is defeated or withdrawn. **p. 48.**

26. What vote and notice are required to rescind?

The motion to rescind requires a majority vote, unless the adopted motion required notice or a higher vote, in which case the same notice and vote are required to rescind the action. **p. 49.**

27. What is the effect of adoption of a motion to rescind?

Adoption of a motion to rescind repeals, cancels, nullifies, or voids the previously adopted motion from the time of adoption of the motion to rescind. **p. 49.**

28. What are the basic rules governing the motion to rescind? Which are different than the rules governing an original (substantive) main motion?

The basic rules governing the specific main motion to rescind are: cannot interrupt a speaker; requires a second; is debatable and opens to debate the motion it proposes to rescind; cannot be amended; requires the same vote (and notice, if any) that was required for adoption of the motion it proposes to rescind; does not take precedence over other motions; applies to main motions adopted at a previous meeting or convention; can have applied to it all subsidiary motions, except the motion to amend, and can have applied to it the incidental motion to withdraw; and cannot be renewed at the same meeting or convention, but can be reconsidered.

The rules that are different than the rules governing an original (substantive) main motion are that it cannot be amended, the vote and notice required for adoption, the rule about the motions to which rescind applies, and the motions which can be applied to the motion to rescind. **p. 49.**

# CHAPTER 9
## Subsidiary Motions

1.   What is the purpose of the motion to amend?

     The purpose of the motion to amend is to modify a motion that is being considered by the assembly so that it will express more satisfactorily the will of the members. **p. 50.**

2.   What are the four types of amendments?

     The four types of amendments are: amendment by inserting (addition), amendment by striking out (deletion), amendment by striking out and inserting, and amendment by substitution. **p. 50.**

3.   What motions may be amended?

     The only motions that may be amended without restriction are main motions (including the specific main motions to ratify and to amend a previous action) and the subsidiary motion to amend. The motions to postpone to a certain time, to limit debate, and to recess may be amended as to time. The motion to refer to a committee may be amended concerning such details as name, number of members, method of selection of the committee, or the instructions to the committee, and such details as the time the motion is to be reported back to the assembly. The privileged motion to adjourn may be amended to change the time of adjournment or to set a time for a continued meeting. **p. 52.**

4.   What is meant by the phrase "must be germane"?

     The phrase "amendments must be germane" means that amendments must be relevant to and have direct bearing on the subject of the pending motion that the amendment seeks to change. **p. 52.**

5.   What is a hostile amendment?  Are hostile amendments in order?

A hostile amendment may be directly opposed to the actual intent of the original motion. It may even nullify or change completely the effect of the motion. Hostile amendments are in order if they are germane to the motion they propose to amend. **p. 53.**

6. What are the limitations on pending amendments?

Only one amendment of each rank can be pending at a time (to any amendable motion). The amendment to the original motion is an amendment of the first rank (or primary amendment). Amendments to a pending amendment are amendments of the second rank (or secondary amendments). Amendments of the third rank are not in order. Amendments of the first rank (primary amendments) must be directly related to the motion to be amended, and amendments of the second rank (secondary amendments) must be directly related to the pending primary amendment. **p. 53.**

7. Are amendments debatable?

Amendments to debatable motions are debatable. Amendments to undebatable motions are not debatable. Debate is limited to the immediately pending amendment, and reference to the main motion (or other motion being amended) is permissible only for the purpose of explaining the amendment or its effect. **p. 54.**

8. What does an amendment by substitution do?

An amendment by substitution rewords the entire original motion. It may be proposed instead of offering multiple amendments to different parts of the original motion, or it may be proposed with entirely different wording, purpose, and effect, as long as it is germane (on the same subject) as the original motion. **pp. 54-55.**

9. How many amendments can a substitution of a new motion have?

A motion to amend by substitution is a primary amendment and therefore is subject only to a secondary amendment. **p. 55.**

10. Explain how a motion or resolution may be amended by filling blanks.

   Motions or resolutions are sometimes submitted with blank spaces for names, dates, or numbers, with the blanks to be filled allowing members, without seconds, to propose suggestions. Sometimes the presiding officer creates a blank by general consent or assumes a blank based on the parliamentary situation. A member may also move to strike out a variable part of a motion to create a blank. The motion to create a blank requires a second and is not debatable. Members then call out suggestions to fill the blank (any words that were stricken to create the blank are automatically a suggestion for filling the blank). When no more suggestions are offered, the presiding officer opens discussion on the suggestions, followed by a vote on each suggestion in the order in which each was proposed. Each member can vote for or against each suggestion, casting as many votes as there are suggestions. The suggestion receiving the highest vote, provided that it is a majority, is inserted in the blank. After the blank is filled, further discussion of the motion or resolution is allowed, after which the presiding officer then takes a vote on the motion as a whole. **pp. 55-56.**

11. When can an amendment be withdrawn?

   The proposer of an amendment has the right to withdraw the amendment at any time before the presiding officer has presented it to the assembly for consideration. As soon as the amendment has been stated to the assembly by the presiding officer, it belongs to the body and the proposer of the amendment can withdraw it only by a vote of the assembly or by general consent. **p. 56.**

12. Explain the process by which someone may suggest a change in wording to a motion that has been proposed, without actually moving to amend it.

A member may suggest a change in wording or an amendment to the proposer of the motion, who may indicate that he or she accepts the new wording. If the original motion has not yet been stated by the presiding officer, the acceptance of the new wording by the proposer is all that is needed, and this incorporates it into the original motion. If the original motion has already been stated by the presiding officer, the new wording or amendment may be incorporated into the motion only by permission of the assembly, which may be granted by general consent. If there is an objection when general consent is requested, the presiding officer states the amendment formally, and it is debated and voted on in the usual manner. **p. 56.**

13.  What does it mean to have "adhering amendments?"

When a main motion that has amendments pending is referred to a committee or postponed to a certain time, all pending amendments adhere to it and go with it. When the main motion comes before the assembly again, the amendments still adhere and are also before the assembly for consideration. **pp. 56-57.**

14.  Explain the method of voting on amendments.

Amendments are voted on in the reverse order of their proposal. An amendment to an amendment (an amendment of the second rank or secondary amendment) is discussed and voted on first; then the amendment of the first rank (primary amendment) is discussed and voted on, and finally the motion to which the amendment was applied. **p. 57.**

15.  What is the vote required for adoption of an amendment?

An amendment to any pending motion or amendment requires only a majority vote to adopt, even if the motion being amended will require a higher vote for its adoption. **p. 57.**

An amendment to the bylaws is a special case of a specific main motion to amend a previous action, and requires the vote (and notice) provided in the bylaws for such amendments, but any amendments to the proposed bylaw amendment require only a majority vote for their adoption. Since the bylaw amendment is a main motion, there may be amendments to it of both the first and second rank. **p. 57.**

16. How can action already taken be amended?

Amending actions previously taken is accomplished by using the specific main motion to amend a previous action, which should not be confused with the subsidiary motion to amend a currently pending main motion. Since the motion to amend a previous action is itself a main motion, it may be amended by both primary and secondary amendments. **pp. 58, 40.**

17. What is the effect of adoption of the motion to amend?

Adoption of the motion to amend changes the original motion as the amendment provides. **p. 58.**

18. What are the basic rules governing the motion to amend?

The basic rules governing the motion to amend are: cannot interrupt a speaker; requires a second; is debatable, unless applied to an undebatable motion; can be amended; requires a majority vote, even if the motion to which it is applies requires a higher vote; takes precedence over the main motion and when applied to other motions, takes precedence over the motion it proposes to amend; applies to motions that may be stated in different ways: main motions, motions that amend a previous action, and motions to ratify, amend, refer to committee, postpone to a certain time, limit debate, recess, and adjourn; can have applied to it the motions to close debate, to limit debate, to amend, and to withdraw; can be renewed at the discretion of the presiding officer. **p. 58.**

19. What is the purpose of a motion to refer to a committee?

The purpose of a motion to refer to a committee is to transfer a motion that is pending before the assembly to a committee for one of the following reasons: to investigate or study the proposal, make recommendations on it, and return it to the assembly; or to conserve the time of the assembly by delegating the duty of deciding the proposal, and sometimes of carrying out the decision, to a smaller group; or to ensure privacy in considering a delicate matter; or to provide a hearing on the proposal. **pp. 58-59.**

20. What provisions may be included in the motion to refer?

A motion to refer may be proposed in the simple form, "I move to refer this motion to a committee," or the member may include provisions such as the type of committee, the number of members and how they are to be selected, the committee chair, or instructions to the committee. If the committee is to have power to take action on behalf of the assembly or the organization, the motion to refer must provide for this power. **pp. 59-60.**

21. If a motion is made to refer a subject to a committee, and no main motion is pending, what kind of motion is this?

A motion to refer a subject or problem to a committee, when no main motion is pending, is a main motion. **p. 60.**

22. What is the effect of adoption of the motion to refer?

The adoption of the motion to refer transfers the main motion and its amendments (if any) to the designated committee immediately. **p. 60.**

23. What are the basic rules governing the motion to refer?

The basic rules governing the motion to refer are: cannot interrupt a speaker; requires a second; debate is restricted to brief discussion on the advisability of referring, and to the committee selected, membership, or duties of the committee, or instructions to it; amendments are restricted to such details as the committee selected, membership, or duties of the committee, or instructions to it; requires a majority vote; takes precedence over the main motion and a motion to amend the main motion; applies to main motions only; can have applied to it the motions to close debate, to limit debate, to amend, and to withdraw; can be renewed after change in the parliamentary situation. **p. 61.**

24.  What is the purpose of a motion to postpone to a certain time?

The purpose of a motion to postpone to a certain time is to put off consideration, or further consideration, of a pending main motion and to fix a definite time for its consideration. **p. 61.**

25.  What are the limitations on a motion to postpone to a certain time?

The motion to postpone to a certain time cannot be used to postpone a main motion to a meeting that is not already scheduled (for example, a special meeting that has not yet been established); cannot be used to postpone a main motion to any time that would be too late for the proposed motion to be effective, if adopted; and cannot be used by delegates at one convention or by members at an annual meeting to postpone to the next convention or annual meeting. **p. 62.**

26.  What are some different ways in which a motion may be postponed to a certain time?

A motion may be postponed to a certain time by designating an actual time, or by designating a particular point in the meeting such as an event, or by designating a future scheduled regular or special meeting. **p. 61.**

A motion may be postponed as a general order, which is the default postponement if nothing is mentioned in the motion to postpone, in which case it is taken up at the designated point in the meeting, but does not interrupt any pending business that is under consideration at that time, instead waiting until that pending business is disposed of. A motion may also be postponed as a special order, which requires that this be specified in the motion to postpone, and which requires a two-thirds vote. A motion postponed as a special order does interrupt any pending business when the designated time arrives, with the pending business completed after the special order is disposed of. **pp. 62-63.**

27. When a motion is postponed to a later meeting, when is it considered?

   If a motion is postponed to a particular meeting but not to a specified time, it comes up under unfinished business at the meeting to which it was postponed. **p. 63**.

28. What happens to a motion that is postponed, but is not taken up at the time or meeting to which it is postponed?

   If a motion is postponed to a later time or event, and is not taken up at the meeting for which it was set, it comes up under unfinished business at the next regular meeting. **p. 64.**

29. What is the effect of adoption of the motion to postpone to a certain time?

   Adoption of the motion to postpone to a certain time puts off consideration of the pending main motion (along with any other pending subsidiary motions) until a certain time, event, date, meeting, or position on the agenda. **p. 64.**

30. What are the basic rules governing the motion to postpone to a certain time?

   The basic rules governing the motion to postpone to a certain time are: cannot interrupt a speaker; requires a second; debate is restricted to brief discussion on reasons for, or time of, postponement; amendments are restricted to the time of postponement, or to making the postponement a special order; requires a majority vote unless proposed as a special order, which requires a two-thirds vote; takes precedence over refer to a committee and amend the main motion; applies to main motions only; can have applied to it the motions to close debate, to limit debate, to amend, and to withdraw; and can be renewed after a change in the parliamentary situation. **pp. 64-65.**

31. What is the purpose of a motion to limit or extend debate?

The purpose of a motion to limit or extend debate relates to the time that will be devoted to discussion of a pending motion or motions. **p. 65.**

32. What are the types of limitations that are usually placed on debate?

The types of limitations placed on debate usually relate to the number of speakers who may participate, the length of time allotted to each speaker, the total time allotted for discussion of the motion, or some variation or combination of these. **pp. 65-66.**

33. What pending motions are affected by the motion to limit or extend debate?

A motion to limit or extend debate may be applied to all pending debatable motions, or to only the immediately pending motion. If the motion to limit or extend debate does not specify the motions to which the limit is to apply, only the immediately pending question is affected. **p. 66.**

34. When is the effect of the motion to limit or extend debate terminated?

A motion limiting or extending debate is in force only during the meeting or convention at which it was adopted. If the main motion is postponed until another meeting, or is referred to a committee, the motion limiting or extending debate is no longer in effect when the motion is taken up again. **p. 66.**

35. What are the basic rules governing the motion to limit debate?

The basic rules governing the motion to limit debate are: cannot interrupt a speaker; requires a second; debate is restricted to type and time of limitations; amendment is restricted to limitations, extensions, or removal of limitations on debate; requires a two-thirds vote because it limits freedom of debate or modifies already adopted limitations on debate; takes precedence over postpone to a certain time, to refer to a committee, to amend the main motion, and to the main motion; applies to debatable motions only; can have applied to it the motions to close debate, to amend and to withdraw; can be renewed after change in the parliamentary situation. **p. 67.**

36. What is the purpose of a motion to close debate and vote immediately?

The purpose of a motion to close debate and vote immediately is to prevent or stop discussion on the pending question or questions, to prevent the proposal of other subsidiary motions except the motion to table the main motion, and to bring the pending question or questions to an immediate vote. **p. 67**.

37. What are some of the restrictions on proposing the motion to close debate and vote immediately?

While the motion to close debate and vote immediately may be proposed at any time after the motion to which it applies has been stated to the assembly, it may not be combined with the motion to which it applies, and it may not be moved by a member at the conclusion of the member's own debate. **p. 68.**

38. How does the motion to close debate and vote immediately affect pending motions?

If the motion to close debate and vote immediately is unqualified it applies to the immediately pending motion only. If applied to more than one pending motion debate may be closed only on successive pending motions and must include the immediately pending motion. The motion to close debate may also be qualified to apply to all pending motions. **p. 68.**

39. What is the effect of adoption of the motion to close debate and vote immediately when qualified to apply to more than

just the immediately pending motion?

If the motion to close debate and vote immediately is qualified to apply to more than just the immediately pending motion, and is adopted, the vote is taken immediately on the immediately pending question, and then, in succession, on all remaining motions on which debate was closed. **p. 68.**

40. How should the presiding officer handle a member who calls out "Call the question" or "Question!"?

If a member calls out "Call the question" or "Question!" (without being recognized) the presiding officer should ignore the member, or call the member to order. If the member first obtains recognition and is clearly attempting to move to close debate and vote immediately, without using the correct form, the presiding officer should assist the member to make the motion correctly. **p. 69.**

41. What are the basic rules governing the motion to close debate and vote immediately?

The basic rules governing the motion to close debate and vote immediately are: cannot interrupt a speaker; requires a second; is not debatable; cannot be amended; requires a two-thirds vote because it prevents or cuts off debate; takes precedence over all subsidiary motions except the motion to table; applies to debatable motions only; can have no motion applied to it except the motion to withdraw; and can be renewed after a change in the parliamentary situation. **p. 70.**

42. What is the purpose of a motion to table?

The purpose of the motion to table is to allow the assembly to dispose of the pending main motion immediately and without further debate, but without a direct vote taken on the pending main motion. **p. 70.**

43. What are the reasons that an assembly may wish to table a main motion?

On occasion, an assembly may wish to dispose of a main

motion without any debate or without further debate and without a direct vote on the main motion, which some members may see as extremely objectionable, divisive, or clearly unwanted. **p. 70.**

44. What happens to adhering motions if a main motion is tabled?

   If a main motion is tabled while other pending motions are adhering, the adhering motions are also tabled and disposed of. **p. 71.**

45. If the assembly wishes to reverse the disposal of the main motion, what may the assembly do?

   If the assembly wishes to reverse the disposal of the main motion, the motion to reconsider the main motion may be used. If the motion to reconsider is adopted, the main motion is returned to consideration by the assembly, but any adhering motions that had been disposed of are not before the assembly. The main motion can also be renewed at a future meeting or convention. **p. 71.**

46. What is the effect of adoption of a motion to table?

   If a motion to table is adopted, debate is stopped on the main motion, and the main motion, and any adhering motions, are removed from the consideration of the assembly during the current meeting or convention. **p. 71.**

47. What are the basic rules governing the motion to table?

   The basic rules governing the motion to table are: cannot interrupt a speaker; requires a second; is not debatable; cannot be amended; requires a two-thirds vote to be adopted; takes precedence over all other subsidiary motions; applies to main motions only; can have no motion applied to it except the motion to withdraw; and cannot be renewed (and cannot be reconsidered, but the main motion that has been tabled can be reconsidered). **p. 72.**

# CHAPTER 10
## Privileged Motions

1.  What is the purpose of a "question of privilege"?

    The purpose of a question of privilege is to allow a single member to request of the presiding officer immediate action that might affect the safety, health, security, comfort, and integrity of the members of the assembly. In some instances the request may be to make a motion to take immediate action even when other business is pending. **p. 73.**

2.  How does the presiding officer handle a question of privilege?

    The presiding officer first must decide if the question of privilege is urgent enough to interrupt the current speaker, if it did interrupt; if not, the presiding officer explains that the privilege will be considered when the speaker who was interrupted has finished. The presiding officer then rules immediately on the question of privilege and grants the request or denies it. If a speaker was interrupted, the speaker is then assigned the floor again. **pp. 74-75.**

3.  What may a member do if the member disagrees with the decision of the presiding officer not to permit a question of privilege or not to grant a request made as a question of privilege?

    The member may appeal the ruling of the presiding officer. **p. 74**.

4.  Explain the difference between a question of privilege of the assembly and a question of personal privilege.

    Questions relating to a privilege of the assembly have to do with the rights, safety, integrity, comfort or convenience of the whole assembly, such as matters dealing with heating, lighting, or control of noise. Questions of personal privilege pertain to an individual member or a small group of members, and usually relate to their rights, reputation, conduct, safety, or convenience as members of the body. **p. 75.**

5.  Explain how motions may be introduced as a question of privilege, and how they are handled.

Sometimes, while one motion is pending, it is necessary to introduce another motion to take care of an emergency. The presiding officer will usually allow the member to propose the motion, and then will decide if it is urgent enough to interrupt business. If the presiding officer believes it needs immediate decision, the question is stated to the assembly and opened for debated, thus setting aside the pending business temporarily. If the presiding officer believes the motion is not urgent or is not a question of privilege, it is ruled not in order until the pending business is disposed of. **p. 75.**

6.  What are the basic rules governing a question of privilege?

The basic rules governing a question of privilege are: can interrupt a speaker if it requires immediate decision and action; no second is required because it is a request; is not debatable because it is decided by the presiding officer; cannot be amended; requires no vote; takes precedence over all motions except to adjourn and to recess; applies to no other motion; can have no motion applied to it except the motion to withdraw; and can be renewed after change in the parliamentary situation. If the question of privilege is stated as a motion and is permitted by the presiding officer, it has all the characteristic of a main motion and is treated in all ways as a main motion. **p. 76.**

7.  What is the purpose of a motion to recess?

The purpose of a motion to recess is to permit a break in a meeting with a definite time for resuming the meeting. **p. 76.**

8.  What is the difference between recess and adjourn?

A motion to recess *interrupts* the current meeting until a later time, and when the assembly reconvenes, the meeting resumes at the point at which it was interrupted by the motion to recess. An unqualified motion to adjourn *terminates* the meeting. When an assembly reconvenes following an unqualified adjournment, it begins an entirely new meeting.

The only exception to this procedure is when an assembly adjourns to a continued meeting. This type of adjournment is, in fact, similar to a recess. **p. 77.**

9.  What are the limitations and restrictions on a motion to recess?

    The duration of a recess is usually brief, but there is no definite limitation on its length, except that a recess cannot extend beyond the time set for the next regular or special meeting or, in a convention, beyond the time set for the next business meeting or for the adjournment of the convention. **p. 77.**

10. What are the basic rules governing the motion to recess?

    The basic rules governing the motion to recess are: cannot interrupt a speaker; requires a second; debate is restricted to a brief discussion on the time, duration, or need for recess; amendments are restricted to the time or duration of the recess; requires a majority vote; takes precedence over all other motions except the motion to adjourn; applies to no other motion; can have applied to it the motions to amend, to withdraw, to limit debate, and to close debate; and can be renewed after change in the parliamentary situation. **p. 78.**

11. What is the purpose of a motion to adjourn?

    The purpose of a motion to adjourn is twofold: (1) to end a meeting or convention, or (2) to end a meeting or convention and to set a time to continue the meeting or convention. p. **78.**

12. When is the motion to adjourn privileged, and when is it not privileged?

    The motion to adjourn is privileged if it is proposed when a main motion is pending. If there is no main motion pending, the motion to adjourn is not privileged, but is a main motion and open to full debate and amendment—it is subject to all the rules of a main motion. **p. 79.**

13. How may the motion to adjourn be debated or amended?

The privileged motion to adjourn may only be debated briefly as to the time or need for adjournment and can be amended to establish a continued meeting or to change the time or place of a proposed continued meeting. The main motion to adjourn may be debated and amended without restriction. **pp. 79, 82.**

14. When a motion to adjourn is made and there is still important business to conduct, what should happen?

When a motion to adjourn has been made and there is still important business to conduct, the presiding officer should call this business to the attention of the assembly before putting the motion to a vote; if the presiding officer fails to do so, any member may call attention to the oversight. After this, the presiding officer would usually ask that the proposer withdraw the motion to adjourn until the essential business has been completed, but if the proposer insists on the motion being considered, it must be voted on, and the assembly has the right to adopt the motion. **pp. 79-80.**

15. When an assembly cannot consider all its important business in the time available for a meeting, what motion should be made?

When an assembly cannot consider all its important business in the time available, it may be desirable to continue the meeting at a later time. The motion to do this may be a privileged motion to adjourn, a main motion to adjourn, or a main motion dealing only with establishing the continued meeting, but the motion must clearly direct that the meeting be continued at another time, and it must specify the time and place of the continued meeting. The continued meeting is actually part of the original meeting, and the interval before it occurs is similar to a recess. **p. 80.**

16. What is the difference between adjournment and dissolution?

An adjournment terminates the current meeting. If there is no provision made for another meeting then a motion to adjourn is, in fact, a motion to dissolve the assembly (but not of the organization, unless the assembly is a mass meeting). If this is so, the presiding officer should call the attention of the assembly to the fact that there is no provision for another meeting and that adoption of the motion to adjourn might dissolve the assembly. A final adjournment that has the effect of dissolving the assembly or closing a convention is termed *adjournment sine die,* or adjournment without day. **p. 80.**

17. Who makes the decision on whether to adjourn?

The assembly makes the decision on whether to adjourn. The presiding officer cannot arbitrarily declare adjournment. However, the after adoption of the motion to adjourn, the presiding officer may make brief announcements and call for brief announcements before declaring the meeting adjourned. The presiding officer may announce adjournment without a vote if no further business is offered when called for. In declaring the adjournment of any meeting, it is good practice for the presiding officer to announce the time and place of the next meeting. **pp. 80-81**.

18. When adjournment has a previously set time, who adjourns the meeting?

When a definite hour for adjournment has been set by the adoption of a program, by rule, or by a previously adopted motion, the presiding officer has the duty to bring this to the attention of the assembly when the hour of adjournment arrives, even if it means interrupting a speaker or the consideration of business. A member may then propose a motion to set another time for adjournment. **p. 81.**

19. What happens to business that is interrupted by adjourn-

ment?

Business interrupted by adjournment comes up as the first item under unfinished business at the next meeting. Business that is interrupted by the final adjournment of a convention is dropped. **p. 81.**

20. What are the basic rules governing the motion to adjourn?

The basic rules governing the motion to adjourn are: cannot interrupt a speaker; requires a second; debate is restricted to a brief discussion on the time or need for adjournment; can be amended to establish a continued meeting or to change the time or place of a proposed continued meeting; requires a majority vote; takes precedence over all other motions when privileged; applies to no other motion; can have no motion applied to it except the motions to amend, to withdraw, to limit debate, and to close debate; and can be renewed after change in the parliamentary situation. **p. 82.**

# CHAPTER 11
## Incidental Motions

1. What is the purpose of a motion to appeal?

   The purpose of a motion to appeal is to enable a member who believes that the presiding officer is mistaken in a ruling to challenge the ruling and have the assembly decide, by vote, whether the presiding officer's decision should be reversed or upheld. **p. 83.**

2. In what situations may an appeal be made?

   Any decision of the presiding officer involving judgment is subject to appeal. The presiding officer's statement of a fact, such as announcing the result of a vote count, or simply answering a question or providing information, such as responding to an inquiry, cannot be appealed. Rulings of the presiding officer related to an unambiguous provision of the bylaws or of the parliamentary authority are not subject to appeal. **p. 83.**

3. When may an appeal be made?

   An appeal can is permissible immediately after the presiding officer's ruling has been rendered. If any other business has been taken up after the ruling, an appeal is not in order. However, if another member has obtained the floor, that member may be interrupted by a member wishing to move an appeal. **p. 84.**

4. How does the presiding officer state the question on an appeal?

   The presiding officer must always state the question on an appeal in the following form: "Those in favor of sustaining the decision of the presiding officer ...." The question on the appeal is stated in a neutral, unbiased, manner, and the appeal must focus on the decision or ruling. **p. 84.**

5.  How does the chair handle debate on an appeal?

    The presiding officer states the reasons for the ruling without leaving the chair. Usually the person who made the appeal would then state his or her reasons for making the appeal. Since an appeal is debatable, any member may debate for or against the ruling. **p. 84.**

6.  What vote is required on an appeal?

    The presiding officer's ruling stands as the decision of the assembly, unless a majority vote reverses the ruling through a motion to appeal the decision. Since the vote is always taken on sustaining the ruling of the presiding officer, the ruling is sustained by either a majority vote or a tie vote; otherwise the ruling is reversed. **pp. 84-85.**

7.  What is the effect of a motion to appeal?

    If the decision of the presiding officer is sustained, the decision becomes the decision of the assembly. If the decision of the presiding officer is not sustained, the decision is reversed. **p. 85.**

8.  What are the basic rules governing the motion to appeal?

    The basic rules governing the motion to appeal are: can interrupt a speaker because it must be proposed immediately after the chair's ruling and before other business has intervened; requires a second; is debatable; cannot be amended; requires a majority vote or a tie vote to sustain the decision of the presiding officer; takes precedence as an incidental motion and must be decided immediately; applies to rulings of the presiding officer; can have applied to it the motions to close debate, limit debate, and to withdraw; and cannot be renewed. **p. 85.**

9.  What is the purpose of the motion to suspend the rules?

The motion to suspend the rules permits an assembly to take some action or permits an action to be taken that otherwise would be prevented by a procedural rule. **p. 85.**

10.  Which rules can be suspended and which rules cannot be suspended?

Only rules of procedure can be suspended. Rules that cannot be suspended include those stated in a statute, charter, or the organization's constitution or bylaws unless a specific provision in these documents of authority provides for suspension of the rule. Also, rules governing notice of meetings or of motions, quorum requirements, special meeting agendas, vote requirements, and voting methods (such as the requirement for a ballot vote) cannot be suspended. **pp. 86-87.**

11.  What are the restrictions and time limits on suspension of rules?

A motion to suspend the rules may be made when no motion is pending, or it may be made when a motion is pending if the suspension is for a purpose connected to that motion. Rules may be suspended only for a specific purpose and only for the limited time necessary to accomplish the proposed action. Any suspension for a longer time would require an amendment of the rules, not a suspension. For this reason the object of the suspension must be specified in the motion to suspend the rules, and only action that is specifically mentioned in the motion to suspend the rules can be taken under the suspension. **p. 87.**

12.  What is the Gordian Knot motion?

The Gordian Knot motion is form of a motion to suspend the rules, used in order to allow some complex and confusing procedural or substantive aspect of the current motion to be resolved. It is usually utilized to begin consideration again at an earlier point in the proceedings that was less confusing or to allow a complicated motion to be reworded without going through all the procedural steps that might otherwise be required. **pp. 87-88.**

13. What is the effect of adopting a motion to suspend the rules?

Adoption of the motion to suspend the rules allows an assembly to take a specific action, within the meeting, that would otherwise be improper under its procedural rules. **p. 89.**

14. What are the basic rules governing the motion to suspend the rules?

The basic rules governing the motion to suspend the rules are: cannot interrupt a speaker; requires a second; is not debatable; cannot be amended; requires a two-thirds vote; takes precedence as an incidental motion and must be decided immediately; applies only to procedural rules and not to another motion; can have no motion applied to it except the motion to withdraw; and can be renewed after a change in the parliamentary situation. **p. 88.**

15. What is the purpose of the motion to consider informally?

The purpose of the motion to consider informally is to allow the assembly to discuss a pending motion with the rules of debate relaxed. The motion also permits a discussion to occur without a pending motion. **p. 89.**

16. What is the effect of adoption of a motion to consider informally?

The adoption of a motion to consider informally while a motion is pending allows the assembly to discuss the motion with the rules of debate relaxed. Length and number of speeches are no longer limited, but rules of decorum, courtesy, and fairness remain in effect. If no motion is pending, adoption of a motion to consider informally allows the assembly to discuss a topic without it being introduced by a motion; such discussion would otherwise not ordinarily be permissible. **p. 89.**

17. What are the basic rules governing the motion to consider informally?

The basic rules governing the motion to consider informally are: cannot interrupt a speaker; requires a second; is not debatable; cannot be amended; requires a majority vote; takes precedence as an incidental motion and must be decided immediately; applies to main motions; can have no motion applied to it except a motion to withdraw; and can be renewed after a change in the parliamentary situation. **p. 89.**

18. What is the purpose of point of order?

A point of order calls the attention of the assembly and of the presiding officer to a violation or potential violation of the rules, an omission, a mistake, or an error in procedure. Its purpose is to secure a ruling from the presiding officer or the assembly on the question raised. Raising a point of order is a demand by a single member that the presiding officer give a ruling or decision on the point raised. **pp. 90-91.**

19. When may a point of order be raised?

A point of order must be raised immediately after the mistake, error, or omission occurs. It cannot be raised later in the meeting, or at another meeting, unless the error involves a violation of law, or a serious violation of the principles of parliamentary procedure or of the bylaws. **p. 91.**

20. How does the presiding officer respond to a point of order?

After clarifying the point being made, if necessary, and after consulting with the parliamentarian or knowledgeable staff members, if necessary, the presiding officer must state that the point of order is well taken (agreeing with the point raised) or is not well taken (disagreeing with the point raised). The ruling on the point of order may be appealed. If the presiding officer is unsure of how to rule because the matter is obscure, or may set an important precedent, the presiding officer may allow the assembly to decide the point.

21. What are the basic rules governing the point of order?

The basic rules governing the point of order are: can interrupt a speaker because a violation of the rules should be corrected immediately; requires no second; is not debatable unless the presiding officer refers it to the assembly for discussion and decision; cannot be amended; requires no vote, as it is decided by the presiding officer, unless the presiding officer refers it to the assembly for discussion and decision by majority vote; takes precedence as an incidental motion and must be decided immediately; applies to any procedural mistake, violation, or omission; can have no motion applied to it except the motion to withdraw; and cannot be renewed. **pp. 92-93.**

22. What is the purpose of an inquiry? What kind of inquiries are there?

An inquiry enables a member to ask the presiding officer a question relating to procedure in connection with a pending motion or with a motion the member may wish to bring before the assembly immediately (parliamentary inquiry), or is a request for substantive information or facts or for information on the meaning or effect of the pending motion from the presiding officer or a speaker (factual inquiry). **p. 93.**

23. To whom is the inquiry addressed?

Inquiries are always addressed to the presiding officer. The presiding officer normally answers a parliamentary inquiry, after consultation with the parliamentarian, if necessary. The presiding officer may answer a factual inquiry, taking care to exhibit no bias on the matter under consideration, or may recognize an officer or staff member, the proposer of the motion, or another member, as appropriate, to provide the requested information. It may not always be possible to provide the answer to a factual inquiry. **p. 95.**

24. May inquiries interrupt a speaker, and if so, what is the ef-

fect of interruption?

An inquiry may interrupt a speaker only if it requires an immediate answer, and the speaker must agree to be interrupted, or may refuse to permit such interruptions. If a speaker is interrupted by an inquiry, and time limits on debate are in effect, the time taken by the question is not deducted from the speaker's time, nor is the time for the answer if the speaker is the one who answers the question. **pp. 95-96.**

25. What are the basic rules governing inquiries?

The basic rules governing inquiries are: can interrupt a speaker only if it requires an immediate answer; requires no second because it is a request; is not debatable; cannot be amended; requires no vote because it is a request and is decided by the presiding officer; takes precedence as an incidental motion and must be decided immediately; applies to any motion; can have no motion applied to it except the motion to withdraw; and cannot be renewed on the same matter. **p. 96.**

26. What is the purpose of a request to withdraw a motion?

A request to withdraw a motion enables a member who has proposed a motion to remove it or request that it be removed from consideration by the assembly. **pp. 96-97.**

27. When can a motion be withdrawn?

Before a motion has been stated by the presiding officer, its proposer may modify or withdraw it without permission of the assembly. Any member, including the presiding officer, may request the maker to withdraw the motion. After the motion has been stated by the presiding officer, the proposer may withdraw it only with the permission of the assembly, which may be granted through a majority vote or by general consent. **pp. 97-98.**

28. How is the motion to withdraw recorded in the minutes?

A motion that is withdrawn after it has been stated by the presiding officer is recorded in minutes with a statement that it was withdrawn. A motion that is withdrawn before the presiding officer states it is not mentioned in the minutes. **p. 98.**

29. What are the basic rules governing the request to withdraw a motion?

The basic rules governing the request to withdraw a motion are: can interrupt a speaker; requires no second because it is a request; is not debatable; cannot be amended; rquires no vote before the motion is stated by the presiding officer, in which case the request is granted, but after the motion is stated by the presiding officer, it requires approval of the assembly by general consent or a majority vote; takes precedence as an incidental motion and must be decided immediately; applies to all motions; can have no motion applied to it; and can be renewed after a change in the parliamentary situation. **p. 98.**

30. What is the purpose of a request for a division of a question?

The purpose of a request for a division of a question is to divide a main motion containing more than one part into individual motions that may be considered and voted on separately. **p. 99.**

31. When are motions divided by the presiding officer, and when are they divided by the assembly?

When a motion contains two or more distinct proposals, each of which is suitable for adoption even if one or more of the other parts is not adopted, a member has the right to request that the motion be divided. If the presiding officer agrees that the motion is divisible, the request should be granted. If the presiding officer believes that there are not distinct proposals that are suitable for individual adoption or defeat, the request may be denied, with an explanation of the reason. If the member disagrees with a denied request, the member may appeal the decision of the presiding officer.

32. What is the purpose of a request to consider a motion by paragraph?

   Parts of a motion may be considered separately when the motion is not easily divisible or when dividing the question may result in ambiguities. In such cases the motion may be considered paragraph by paragraph or section by section. The various paragraphs are not independent and are not treated as separate motions, but each paragraph is debated and amended separately, after which the entire motion is open to further debate and amendment, after which it is voted on as a whole. The value of this approach is to focus the attention of the assembly on one paragraph or section at a time. **pp. 100-101.**

33. When may a division of a question be proposed?

   Division of a question may be proposed at any time before the vote has begun. However, it is most effective if the request to divide the question is made immediately after the introduction of the motion to be divided. **p. 101.**

34. What are the basic rules governing the request for a division of a question or for consideration by paragraph?

   The basic rules governing the request for a division of the question or for consideration by paragraph are: cannot interrupt a speaker; requires no second if granted by the presiding officer as a request, but requires a second if offered as a motion; is not debatable; cannot be amended; requires no vote if granted by the presiding officer as a request, but requires a majority vote  if offered as a motion; takes precedence as an incidental motion and must be decided immediately; applies to main motions only; can have no motion applied to it except the motion to withdraw; and can be renewed after a change in the parliamentary situation. **pp. 101-102.**

35. What is the purpose of the call for a division of the as-

sembly?

A call for a division of the assembly permits the assembly to verify an indecisive voice vote or an indecisive show of hands vote by requiring members to rise, and, if necessary, to be counted. The presiding officer should take the initiative in calling for a standing vote, and a counted vote if necessary, whenever there is any doubt as to the outcome of the vote. **pp. 102-103.**

36.  When may a division of the assembly be requested?

Any member, without waiting for recognition, may call for a division as soon as a question has been put to the vote and even before the vote is announced. The right to call for a division continues after the vote is announced and another speaker has claimed the floor (but has not begun speaking). **p. 102.**

37.  What are the basic rules governing the call for a division of the assembly?

The basic rules governing the call for a division of the assembly are: can interrupt proceedings because it requires immediate decision; requires no second; is not debatable; cannot be amended; requires no vote, unless the presiding officer's denial of a counted division is unsatisfactory to a member (see **p. 103**); takes precedence as an incidental motion and must be decided immediately; applies to an indecisive voice or hand vote; can have no motion applied to it; and cannot be renewed. **pp. 103-104.**

# CHAPTER 12
## Types of Meetings

1.    Define a meeting.

      A meeting is an official assembly of the members of an organization or board during which the member remain together in one place except when there is a recess. It covers the period from the time the group convenes until the time it adjourns. **p. 105.**

2.    Define a convention.

      A convention usually refers to a series of meetings that follow in relatively close succession. It is regarded as a single meeting with intervening recess periods, some of which may be from day to day. **p. 105.**

3.    What is a regular meeting?

      A regular meeting of an organization or board is one of a series of meetings for which the dates and sometimes location are established in the bylaws or set by adoption of a motion. **p. 105.**

4.    What is a special meeting?

      A special meeting is a meeting that is not regularly scheduled and is held to transact specified business as stated in the call of the meeting. Any special meeting of an organization or a board must be called in accordance with bylaw provisions governing special meetings or in accordance with applicable statutory requirements. **p. 106**.

5.    When are minutes of a special meeting read?

      Minutes of the special meeting are read and approved at the next regular meeting. **p. 107.**

---

6. .How is a continued meeting defined?

   A continued meeting is a legally a continuation of the original meeting. It is set for a date, time, and place as determined by the motion that created the meeting. **p. 107**.

7. Under what type of meeting do boards and committees operate?

   Boards and committees are normally considered to operate in a closed meeting unless the organization documents are state otherwise. **p. 108.**

8. List some rules to be used when some members are grouped together in one location with others participating at individual locations.

   Rules for recognizing members to speak, for taking a vote, and for ensuring that only members attend. **p. 109.**

9. List some basic rules that must be established for meetings in which members are not in the same place.

   A quorum is established through a roll call; members always state their names before speaking; at the presiding officer's discretion, discussion takes place on a rotating basis; and votes are taken by roll call or by general consent. **p. 109**.

# CHAPTER 13
## Notice of Meetings and Proposals

1.  Why is notice important?

    The courts will not uphold the decisions of a meeting if the notice requirements for the meeting, or for any action that requires notice, have not been complied with. If there is proof that notice of a meeting is purposely or negligently withheld from any member, actions taken at that meeting are not valid. . . . Notice of a meeting sent so late that a substantial number of members cannot attend is not a valid notice, even if all other requirements have been met. **pp. 111, 112, 311.**

2.  What should a notice of meeting contain?

    The call must give notice of the exact time of calling the meeting to order; the place of the meeting; and any additional information that would assist the members in preparing for the meeting. **p. 112**.

3.  How are convention notices most often issued?

    They are most often issued in the form of a call to the convention.
    The call must give notice of the exact time and place of the convention and usually includes the method of accrediting delegates and directions for sending resolutions, reports of officers and committees, and proposed amendments to the bylaws. The call is usually sent by letter or electronic means, or is printed in the organization's magazine. A call can be in the form of a notice or a greeting, or in any form that makes it clear that a convention is being called and when and where the convention will be held. **p. 112.**

4.  What should notice of a special meeting contain?

It should contain the time and place, and also notice of specific proposals to be considered and decided, and of subjects to be discussed. **p. 113.**

5.   Do continued (adjourned) meetings require notice?

*Continued meetings* (that is, meetings that are a resumption of meetings that were adjourned to a particular hour or date) do not require notice unless this requirement is in the organization's governing documents. If either a regular or a special meeting that has been properly called votes to adjourn to a later time to continue the meeting, this is sufficient notice to those present. However, good organizational practice requires that notice of the continued meeting be sent to all members. **p. 113.**

6.   List the two ways a member may waive notice?

A member may waive notice if the member attends a meeting for which he did not receive notice (or received an erroneous notice) and participates in the meeting and does not protest lack of notice. The member may also waive notice by signing a written waiver of notice before, during, or after the meeting. **p. 114.**

7.   In a proposal that is required by law, charter, or by a provision in the bylaws to be given notice, how should the proposal be stated in the call to the meeting?

The proposal to be voted on must be stated specifically. **p. 113.**

8.   If the organization's bylaws set the number of members of the board at 13 and notice was given to reduce the number to 9 members, what amendments to the proposal would be permitted?

Amendments to motion must fall within the scope of the notice given. For example, if an organization's bylaws set the number of members of the board at 13 and notice was given to reduce the board to 9 members, any amendment specifying a future between 9 and 13 would be in order, but an amendment increasing the number of members to over 13 or reducing the number of board members below 9, would be out of order. **p. 114.**

This page intentionally left blank.

# CHAPTER 14
## Order of Business and Agenda

1.   What is an order of business?

     An order of business is a blueprint for meetings. It is a defined sequence of the different sections of business covered in the order in which each will be called up during business meetings. **p. 115.**

2.   What is the common parliamentary law pattern for an order of business?

     If the bylaws or standing rules do not include an order of business, parliamentary law has established the following pattern: call to order; reading, correction, approval, or disposition of minutes of previous meetings; reports of officers; reports of boards and standing committees; reports of special committees; unfinished business; new business; announcements; and adjournment. **p. 115.**

3.   Where is a prayer, opening ceremony, or roll call included in an order of business?

     These items, when required, should follow the call to order and precede the other items of business. **p. 115.**

4.   What is the order of business for a special meeting?

     The order of business for a special meeting consists only of the call to order, consideration of the items of business stated in the notice of the meeting, and adjournment. **p. 116.**

5.   What is the order of business for a convention?

     The order of business for a convention should be prepared to fulfil the particular needs of the organization and its members. When a program or schedule for a business meetings has been adopted by a convention and a time has been fixed for considering certain items of business, this schedule cannot be deviated from, except by general consent or by majority vote. **p. 116.**

6. What is an agenda?

An agenda is a list of the specific items under each division of an order of business that the members agree to consider in a meeting. **pp. 115, 116.**

7. How is the postponement of reading of the minutes handled?

The reading of the unapproved minutes may be postponed to a certain time or to a subsequent meeting by a general consent or by majority vote, although this generally is not advisable. If the reading of the minutes of several previous meetings has been postponed to the current meeting, the agenda should list them in chronological order for approval. **p. 117.**

8. What action is taken on the treasurer's report?

No action by the assembly is required on a treasurer's report. After any questions, the report is filed. **p. 118.**

9. What does unfinished business contain?

Unfinished business includes only two types of items. First, any motion or report that was being considered and was interrupted when the previous meeting adjourned. Second, any motion or report that was postponed to the current meeting except those which have been set for a particular hour on the agenda. **p. 118.**

10. What does new business contain?

New business includes any proposal that any member may wish to present to the assembly, except items of business that must be presented under other divisions of the order of business. **p. 119.**

11. Why should "announcements" be part of the order of business?

A meeting is expedited by having a regular place in the order of business for announcements. After making announcements, the presiding officer may call for announcements from members. **p. 119.**

12. Who adjourns the meeting?

The presiding officer formally ends the meeting by declaring it adjourned.
The presiding officer cannot, without a formal vote or general consent, declare the meeting adjourned if any member wishes to bring up additional business. The decision on whether to adjourn is made by the members. **pp. 119-120.**

13. In a convention, when a program has been adopted and a time fixed for considering certain items of business, how may the schedule of business items be deviated from?

Unless the organization has a rule to the contrary, the use of an adopted agenda does not preclude other items of business from being added, deleted, or moved around on the agenda during the meeting. **p. 120.**

14. What is a consent agenda?

Organizations having a large number of routine or noncontroversial matters to approve can save time by use of a *consent agenda*, also called a *consent calendar*. This is part of the printed agenda listing matters that are routine or expected to be noncontroversial and on which there are likely to be no questions or discussion. **p. 120.**

15. What is the procedure for removing an item from the consent agenda for separate consideration?

A single member has a right to remove any item from the consent agenda, in which case it is transferred to the regular agenda so that it is considered and voted on separately. A member may ask a question to clarify a consent agenda item without removing it from the consent agenda, but if this proves to be more than a clarification, the presiding officer can insist that it be removed and placed on the regular agenda. **pp. 120-121.**

16. How is a consent agenda established? consideration?

During a meeting, the chair or any member may propose that a consent calendar be established for certain items on the agenda to permit them to be voted *en bloc*. The organization can adopt a special rule to determine who shall establish the consent agenda. **p. 121.**

17. What is a priority agenda?

A priority agenda allows a meeting to take up important agenda items, or business of significant consequence, early in the meeting. This is useful when there are many items of business and limited time for their consideration. The items of business in the priority agenda are taken up after the consent agenda is disposed of. **p. 121.**

# CHAPTER 15
## Quorum

1.    Define a quorum.

     A quorum is the minimum number or minimal proportion of the members of an organization that must be present at a meeting in order to transact business legally.  p. **122.**

2.    What is the quorum requirement for a regular meeting, a mass meeting, a convention, boards and committees?

     Regular meeting: The bylaws of an organization should state, as a minimum the number of proportion of members that constitute the quorum of a board meeting and meetings of members. In the absence of such a bylaws clause or applicable statutory provision, under parliamentary law: (1) in the case of membership organizations with a verifiable roll of members, the quorum is fixed as a majority of the voting members, and (2) in the case of organizations with an indefinite number of members, such as a some churches or neighbourhood groups that do not charge dues, the voting members who attend the meeting, however few in number, constitute a quorum.

     The number required for a quorum should be small enough to ensure that a quorum usually will be present but large enough to protect the organization against decisions by a small minority of the members. **p. 122.**

     Mass meeting. A mass meeting (organizing meeting) of an organization without a definite membership considers the members present, no matter what their numbers, as the quorum. **p. 123.**

     Convention: In conventions where the business of the organization is transacted by delegates who are expected to be present at all business meetings, the required quorum should be higher—example, a majority of the delegates registered as at the convention. **p. 123.**

Boards and Committees: In boards and committees, the quorum is a majority of the members then in office unless set at a different level in the organization's rules of statute. **p. 123.**

3. What does a quorum refer to?

A quorum always refers to the number of members *present*, not to the number *voting*. If a quorum is present, a vote is valid even if fewer members than the number specified as present participate in the vote. **p. 123.**

4. In computing a quorum, who is counted?

In computing a quorum, only members present and in good standing are counted. **p. 124.**

5. Does a member with a personal interest in a question affect the quorum?

Organizations should look to applicable law in their jurisdiction to ensure compliance with the quorum requirements and especially where a member has declared a personal interest in a question currently before the body. In organizations adopting this book as their parliamentary authority, a member with a personal interest may not vote or debate on the issue, but if present, is counted toward unless the bylaws of the organization or applicable law requires otherwise. **p. 124.**

6. What does the term "in good standing" mean?

The meaning of the phrase "in good standing" varies with different organizations according to their bylaws. **p. 124.**

7. Whose duty is it to raise a question on quorum?

It is the duty of the presiding officer to notify the assembly any time is becomes apparent that a quorum is not present. If the presiding officer fails to do so, any member who doubts that a quorum is present at a particular time during a meeting has the right to rise to a point of order and request that the members be counted (called a *quorum count)*. **p. 124.**

8.      How is the presence of a quorum determined?

The presence of quorum is determined by counting the members present or by calling the roll. **p. 124.**

9.      When is a quorum presumed to be present?

It is presumed that since the minutes show that a quorum was present when the meeting began, a quorum continued to be present until recess or adjournment. **p. 125.**

This page intentionally left blank.

# CHAPTER 16
## Debate

1.     How is debate regulated?

    Debate is regulated by parliamentary rules in order to assure every member a reasonable and equal opportunity to be heard. **p. 126.**

2.     What is the extent of debate on motions?

    Motions may be fully debatable, or debatable with restrictions, or not debatable. **p. 126.**

3.     What motions are fully debatable?

    The following motions require full or unlimited debate for their decision: main motions, to amend a previous action, to rescind, to ratify, to amend (unless applied to an undebatable motion), to adopt in-lieu-of, and to appeal. **p. 126.**

4.     What motions are debatable with restrictions?

    There are eight motions that are debatable with restrictions: the privileged motions to adjourn and to recess; the subsidiary motions to limit debate to postpone to a certain time, to refer to a committee, and to amend a motion for which debate is restricted; and the specific main motions to recall a motion or subject from a committee (or board) and to reconsider. **p. 127.**

5.     What motions are not debatable?

    All motions, other than those specified in 3 and 4 above, are not debatable and must be put to a vote immediately. **p. 127.**

6.     How does a member obtain the floor?

A member obtains the floor by waiting until no one has the floor, then rises, addresses the presiding officer, and waits for recognition. **p. 127.**

7.   When several seek recognition at the same time, how does the presiding officer decide which member should be recognized?

The presiding officer is guided by the following rules when several members seek recognition: (1) the person or the committee person who presented a motion or report should be allowed the first opportunity to explain the motion or report, and is usually given the opportunity to speak again when it appears that all others who wish to do so have spoken; ; (2) a member who has not spoken on the immediate pending motion has prior claim over one who has already spoken, and a member who seldom speaks should be given preference over a member who frequently speaks; and (3) the presiding officer should attempt to alternate between the proponents and opponents of a motion. **pp. 127-128.**

8.   When may a person speak more than once?

If no other member seeks recognition, a member who has already spoken may be recognized to speak again. No member or a small number of members should not be permitted to dominate debate to the extent that only one side of the issue is presented. **p. 128.**

9.   What is NOT debate?

A brief comment or remark by the proposer of a motion before stating it is generally permissible. Similarly, a very brief explanatory remark or a question is sometimes permitted on an undebatable motion. An inquiry, or a brief suggestion or explanation, is not debate. **pp. 128-129.**

10.   How is relevancy in debate determined?

Discussion that departs from the subject under discussion or the pending question is out of order because it is not germane or relevant to the proposal. **p. 129.**

11.  What is meant by "dilatory tactics"?

Dilatory tactics are those actions that delay the proposal or the vote on a subject by making unnecessary motions, asking pointless questions, or talking around and not on the question. Such tactics are always out of order. **p. 130.**

12.  How should a member conduct himself during debate?

Debate must be impersonal, addressed through the presiding officer, and never directed to an individual. The motion, not the advocate, is the subject of debate. **p. 130.**

13.  What are the presiding officer's duties during debate?

The presiding officer has the responsibility of controlling and expediting debate. A member who has been given the floor has a right to undivided attention of the assembly. It is the duty of the presiding officer to protect the speaker in this right by suppressing disorder, by eliminating whispering and walking about, and by preventing annoyance, heckling or unnecessary interruptions. The presiding officer should insist that every member be attentive to the business before the assembly. It is also the presiding officer's duty to keep the subject clearly before the members, to rule out irrelevant discussion, and to restate the motion when necessary. **p. 131.**

14.  What are the time limits on debate?

Parliamentary law fixes no limit on the length of speeches during debate. Each organization has the right to establish limits on debate if the members wish to do so. **p. 131.**

15.  How is a question brought to a vote?

When it appears that all members who wish to speak have done so, the presiding officer inquiries, "Is there any further discussion?" If there is no further discussion, the presiding officer should take the vote on the pending question. **p. 132.**

16.  How is informal consideration brought about?

A member may move to consider a particular motion, subject, or problem informally. **pp. 89, 133.**

17.  How is informal consideration terminated?

(1) By offering a motion embodying the idea that was being considered informally. **p. 133.**
(2) By the members deciding to take a vote on the motion being considered informally or by adopting another permissible motion such as an amendment, referral, or postponement. **p. 134.**

# CHAPTER 17
## Votes Required for Valid Action

1.   What is the significance of a majority vote?

     One of the fundamental concepts in a democracy is that the ultimate authority lies in a majority of the citizens of the democracy. Likewise in an organization, the ultimate authority lies in a majority of the members when they meet to take action through majority votes. Thomas Jefferson said, "Until a majority has spoken, nothing has changed." To permit less than a majority to decide for any group would subject the many to the rule of the few, and this would be contrary to the most basic democratic principle. **p. 135.**

2.   What is the meaning of "majority vote" as it is used in *AIPSC*?

     A "majority vote" in *AIPSC*, unless otherwise qualified, is defined as a majority of the legal votes cast by members present and voting. **p. 135.**

3.   Under what circumstances may a proposal or an election be decided other than by majority vote?

     Any requirement permitting decisions by less than a majority vote (for example, by plurality as in an election) or requiring more than a majority vote (for example, a two-thirds vote on a substantive proposal) are not valid unless they are included in a statute, the charter, or in the bylaws. **p. 136.**

4.   What happens when more than a majority vote is required?

     Sometimes members mistakenly assume that the higher the vote required for taking an action, the more democratic the process is and that it provides for greater protection of members' rights. The opposite is true. Whenever a vote of more than a majority is required to take action, control is taken from the majority and given to a minority. **p. 136.**

5.  What is the exception to the principle of requiring only a majority vote?

    One exception to the principle of requiring only a majority vote is when the vote has an adverse impact on the rights of the members. Another exception is when the rights of absentees are involved. **p. 137.**

6.  Where should vote requirements be defined?

    Every organization should state in its bylaws the vote required for election of candidates and also the vote required for important decisions. Whenever the basis on which a vote must be computed is not defined in statute, charter, or bylaws, it is a majority of the legal votes cast by members present and voting. **p. 138.**

7.  List various ways that a majority vote can be computed.

    A majority vote, or any other vote, may be qualified or defined in many ways. A majority vote could be variously computed as: a majority of all the membership positions; a majority of the members in good standing; a majority of the members present; a majority of a quorum; a majority of the legal votes cast **p. 138.**

8.  What is meant by "a majority vote of all the members in good standing"?

    A majority vote of all the members in good standing means a vote of more than half of all the members both present and absent. **p. 138.**

9.  The bylaws state that a certain class of motions must be adopted by at least a majority of the quorum. The quorum is 100 members. What is the minimum number of members required to vote in the affirmative to adopt a motion in this class of motions?

A minimum of 51 members will be required to vote in the affirmative (and to be a majority of the legal votes cast. **p. 139.**

10. Why are abstentions not counted?

   An abstention is not considered a vote and is therefore not counted in determining the result. A member who abstains has in fact relinquished his or her vote... A member has the right to abstain from voting on any motion, and must abstain from voting if the member has a financial interest of conflict of interest in the outcome of the vote. **p. 140.**

11. What is a plurality vote?

   A plurality vote means more votes than the number received by any other candidate or alternative proposition. There is no requirement in plurality voting that a candidate or any proposition receive a majority vote. **p. 140.**

12. When can a candidate be elected by plurality vote?

   A plurality vote does not elect a candidate except when the bylaws provide for a decision by plurality vote. **p. 140.**

13. What is unanimous vote?

   A unanimous vote on a proposal is a vote in which all the legal votes cast are on the same side, whether affirmative or negative. A unanimous vote for a particular office is a vote in which one candidate receives all the legal votes cast for that office. **p. 141.**

14. What is a tie vote?

   A tie vote on a *motion* means that the same number of members has voted in the affirmative as in the negative... An equal or tie vote means that the motion is defeated. When a tie vote between two or more candidates in an election results in a deadlock, the vote must be retaken until the tie is resolved. **p. 142.**

15.   When does the presiding officer vote?

The presiding officer customarily votes in an assembly only when the vote is by ballot or when his or her vote will make a difference in the result. **p. 142.**

16.   What is a simple formula for computing a two-thirds vote?

Doubling the negative vote attained gives the minimum number of votes required to adopt a motion requiring a two-thirds vote. If the affirmative vote is equal to or higher than the negative vote doubled, the proposal has obtained the necessary two-thirds vote and is adopted. Otherwise, it is lost. **p. 143.**

17.   When officers of equal rank are being voted on simultaneously and require a majority vote, what are the minimum requirements for election?

The nominee must receive a majority vote based on the total number of ballots cast for all of the equal offices; and among those candidates receiving such a majority vote, those receiving the highest vote are declared elected. **p. 144.**

18.   What is meant by a double majority?

A double majority means that a majority of the individual members and a majority of the caucuses must vote in favor of the proposal for it to be adopted. **p. 145.**

19.   When can a member NOT vote?

As a general principle, a member having a direct personal or financial interest in a matter should not vote on it... A member may vote on a question involving the whole organization when others are equally affected by the vote, even though the member has a direct personal or financial interest... When charges have been made against a member, that member cannot vote on the charges. **p. 146.**

# CHAPTER 18
## Methods of Voting

1. What is a vote?

   In an assembly, a vote is a formal expression of the will of the assembly. **p. 147.**

2. What are the usual methods of voting?

   There are five usual methods of voting: general consent, voice vote, standing vote or show of hands, roll call, and ballot. **p. 147.**

3. What is general consent and when is it appropriate to use this voting method?

   Routine or noncontroversial questions are often decided by general consent—without taking a formal vote. When members are in general agreement, this method (sometimes called unanimous consent) saves time and expedites business. **p. 148.**

4. If the presiding officer tries to take a vote by general consent and a member wishes to take a vote, what should the member say?

   If any member says, "I object," a vote must be taken on the motion. **p. 148.**

5. If a member believes a vote is indecisive, what should the member do?

   Any member who believes that a vote is indecisive or that the presiding officer has not announced it correctly my interrupt, if necessary, and call for a division of the assembly to verify the vote. This right continues even after the vote has been announced and another speaker has claimed the floor, but the right must be exercised before the speaker has begun to speak. **p. 148.**

6.  If a motion appears to be adopted unanimously, may the presiding officer dispense with taking the negative vote? Is there an exception?

    No. The negative vote must always be called for, even if the affirmative vote appears to be overwhelming or unanimous. The only exception is a courtesy vote. **p. 148.**

7.  Explain how a roll call vote is taken.

    The presiding officer states the question on the roll call as follows: "The motion is . . . . Those in favor of the motion will vote aye (or yea) as their names are called; those opposed will vote no (or nay). The secretary will call the roll." The names are called in alphabetical order or some other appropriate order. The name of the presiding officer is usually called last. A member who does not wish to vote may remain silent or answer "present" or "abstaining." **p. 150.**

8.  When can an organization use voting by mail?

    Voting by mail cannot be used unless it is authorized in the bylaws. **p. 152.**

9.  What are the advantages and disadvantages of voting by mail?

    In organizations whose members are scattered over a wide area or who work during different hours of the day, provision is sometimes made for members to vote on important questions by mail. Voting by mail has certain disadvantages. When voting by mail, the members do not have the opportunity to discuss oe listen to debate on proposals or to amend proposals. In elections, there is no opportunity to nominate candidates from the floor. **p. 152.**

10. What is the advantage of electronic voting?

Thousands of ballots can be tabulated in several minutes. **p. 153.**

11.   What is a proxy?

A proxy is a written authorization empowering another person to act, in a meeting, for the member who signs the proxy. ... The term *proxy* may mean either the statement authorizing another to act in place of the member signing it, or it may refer to the person who attends the meeting in place of the absent member. **pp. 153-154.**

12.   Can proxies be used to establish a quorum?

If an organization uses proxies, the bylaws should specify whether they count toward establishing a quorum. **p. 155.**

13.   Describe *AIPSC*'s default preferential voting system.

In an election using *AIPSC*'s default preferential voting system, members mark their ballots to indicate their first, second, third, and subsequent choices among the candidates. Tellers count the ballots and report the results based on first-choice votes only, and if no candidate receives a majority of the votes on this basis, the candidate with the fewest first-choice votes is dropped, and the ballots that voted for that person are recounted, based on second-choice votes. These votes are added to the original totals. If no candidate has a majority after this (or any subsequent) count, the process is repeated, dropping the lowest candidate and distributing that candidate's first-choice votes among the remaining candidates until one has received a majority vote. **p. 156.**

14.   What is a Borda Count method?

The Borda Count method of voting is not a majority voting system; it is based on a point system. The tellers committee will tally all the points for each candidate. The candidate with the most points is elected. **p. 157.**

15.　When may a member change his vote?

When a vote is taken by voice, a show of hands, standing, or by roll call, members may change their votes up to the time that the result of the vote is announced. After a vote by roll call has been announced, a member may change a vote only with proof that an error was made in recording it. When voting is by ballot, a member may not change the ballot after it has been placed in the ballot box. **p. 157.**

16.　What is a straw vote? Is it a binding vote if taken during a meeting? Why?

A straw vote is an improper practice of taking an informal test in meetings, which they interpret to be a vote that is not binding. . . . No body, board, or committee can, during its meeting, properly take a vote that is not binding. Under the law, all votes taken during a meeting are binding. **p. 158.**

# CHAPTER 19
## Nominations and Elections

1.  What should the bylaw provisions on nominations contain?

    The bylaw provision on nominations should include the offices to be filled, the eligibility and qualification of candidates, the person or group who may nominate, the method and time of nominating, and the term of office. If a nominating committee is to be used, provisions for selecting its members and determining their qualifications, instructions, duties, and reporting requirements should also be included. **p. 159.**

2.  What should the bylaw provision on elections contain?

    The bylaw provision on elections should contain the time, place, and method of voting; the notice required; a statement of who is eligible to vote; the vote required to elect; the method of conducting the election; and the time when the new officers take office. Some bylaws include a provision for special elections if needed to fill vacancies. **p. 159.**

3.  What is a nomination?

    A nomination is the formal presentation to an assembly of the name of a member as a candidate for a particular office. **p. 160.**

4.  Are nominations from the floor always permitted?

    Unless the bylaws provide otherwise, nominations from the floor are always permitted even if the initial nominations are made by a nominating committee. **p. 160.**

5.  Is relying solely on nominations from the floor a good method?

Relying solely on nominations from the floor is often not the most satisfactory method for securing the best candidates. The lack of time for considering qualifications, the tendency of nominees to decline nominations from the floor, and the resulting confusion often prevent the organization from securing the best leaders. A nominating committee, so long as it is fairly chosen and is representative of the membership, will usually select good candidates, but nominations from the floor should always be provided as a safeguard. **p. 160.**

6.   How are nominations from the floor closed?

The presiding officer should repeat the request for further nominations and should pause to allow ample opportunity for members to present nominees. When there appear to be no further nominations for a particular office, the presiding officer may declare nominations for that office closed. A motion to close nominations is not required but, if made, is unamendable and undebatable and requires a two-thirds vote for adoption. The presiding officer should not recognize a motion to close nominations or declare them closed if any member is rising for the purpose of making a nomination. **pp. 160-161.**

7.   By what means may a member, who was not nominated by a committee or from the floor, be elected?

Unless the bylaws require a nomination, members may vote for anyone who is eligible, regardless of whether the person has been nominated by writing the name of their choice on the ballot or voting for that person during roll call. Any member receiving the necessary vote is elected, whether nominated or not. **p. 161.**

8.   What are some reasons for the selection of a nominating committee?

A nominating committee is one of the most important committees of an organization because it can help secure the best officers. . . . A committee has the time to study the current leadership needs of the organization and to select candidates to meet those needs. The committee can interview prospective nominees; investigate their expertise, qualifications, and abilities; persuade them to become candidates; and secure their consent to serve if elected. The committee is also able to apportion representation equitably among different groups and different geographical areas. **p. 161.**

9.  How is a nominating committee selected?

    A nominating committee should be a representative committee....When possible, the committee should represent the demographics of the whole organization. Any plan in which experienced leaders choose some of the members of the nominating committee and the membership chooses the other members is usually effective in securing a committee that is both representative and knowledgeable. ... When a nominating committee is used, it is essential that the members be chosen wisely and democratically and that both the committee and the membership be protected by permitting nominations from the floor. **pp. 161-162.**

10. Which member of the board should NOT be on the nominating committee?

    The president, president-elect, and immediate past president should not appoint any members of the nominating committee, serve on the committee, give the committee instructions, or take any part in its deliberations. **p. 162.**

11. What are the duties usually assigned to a nominating committee?

    The duties usually assigned to a nominating committee are: to select nominees whose experience and qualities meet the needs of the organization; to contact prospective nominees and obtain their consent to serve if elected; and to prepare and submit a report, which may include the reasons for the selection of the nominees. **p. 162.**

12. Where are the qualifications of nominees listed?

Qualifications for each office should be stated in the bylaws or other document of authority as designated in the bylaws, such as a policy established by the board or by the members. **p. 163.**

13. Can a member become a candidate for another office without giving up his or her   currently held office?

Unless the bylaws state otherwise, a member who holds an office may be a candidate for another office, without first giving up his or her current office, but if the member is elected to and accepts an incompatible office, the current office is forfeited. **p. 163.**

14. May members of the nominating committee become candidates?

Members who are likely to become candidates should not serve on a nominating committee, but members of the committee can become candidates. A member of a nominating committee who becomes a candidate should resign from the committee immediately. **p. 163.**

15. Should an organization require a multiple slate of nominees?

For a number of reasons, it is usually not best practice to require the nominating committee to submit more nominations than there are positions to be filled. ...If a fully qualified candidate is selected, but the governing documents of the organization require two nominees, the committee may find itself in the position of finding a "throwaway" candidate to fill the second position. A member nominated only to fulfill the requirement may be unwilling to run in the future after having been defeated once. **p. 164**.

16. Who should serve on an election committee?

The members of the committee should be well respected in the organization, not openly supportive of any one candidate, detail-oriented, thoroughly knowledgeable of the election rules, and if possible, selected from different constituencies or geographic regions. Members of the nominating committee should not serve on the the election committee because of their involvement in the nominating process. **p. 164.**

17. Who has a right to observe the counting of ballots?

   Announced candidates or their delegates have a right to attend and observe the vote count. **p. 165.**

18. List some rules governing the legality of ballots.

   The legality of ballots is governed by the following rules: a mistake in voting for a candidate for one office does not invalidate the vote for candidates for other offices on the same ballot; a technical error, such as a misspelling or using a cross instead of a check mark, does not invalidate a ballot if the *intent* of the voter is clear; a torn or defaced ballot is valid if the *intent* of the voter is clear; votes for ineligible persons are considered illegal ballots; blank ballots are ignored (they are not counted and do not affect the number necessary to elect a candidate or adopt a proposal); and if several nominees for equal offices are voted for in a group, a ballot containing fewer votes than the number of positions to be filled is valid (but a ballot containing votes for more than the number of position to be filled is illegal). **p. 166.**

19. Give the requirements of a report of an election committee.

   The report must account for all ballots cast, both legal and illegal. Blank ballots need not be reported. If any ballots or votes are rejected as illegal, the number must be reported and the reason for rejection must be given. The number of votes received by each candidate and the number of write-in votes for any member, qualified or unqualified, must be included in the report and must be read. The chair of the election committee reads the report without stating who is elected and hands it to the presiding officer. The presiding officer reads to the assembly only the names of those who are elected and declares them elected. **p. 168.**

20. What vote is necessary to elect?

   The vote necessary to elect should be fixed in the bylaws. Unless otherwise stated, the following rules govern: a candidate who receives a majority of the legal votes cast for a single office is elected; a candidate who receives a plurality of the legal votes cast, but not a majority, is not elected unless there is a provision in the bylaws for election by plurality; when an election to an office requires a majority vote but no candidate receives a majority vote, the requirement for a majority vote cannot be waived, but the assembly may adopt motions to enable it to complete the election within a reasonable time. **p. 168.**

21. When does an election become effective?

   An election becomes effective immediately if the candidate is present and does not decline. Election of a candidate who is absent and has consented to the nomination becomes effective as soon as the person is notified and agrees to serve. Unless some other time is specified in the bylaws, a person assumes office when declared elected, and no formal installation is necessary. Often, the bylaws provide that the new officers should take office at a specific time. **p. 170.**

22. When may an election be challenged?

   An election may be challenged only during the time that it is taking place or within a reasonably brief time thereafter. Unless an organization provides special procedures for challenging an election, elections may not be challenged after the adjournment of the election meeting or convention, unless the election challenge is based on fraudulent activity. **p. 170.**

# CHAPTER 20
## Officers

1.   *American Institute of Parliamentarians Standard Code of Parliamentary Procedure (AIPSC)* states that the president or the head of an organization, whatever the title may be, has three roles. What are they?

     The *president*, the head of an organization regardless of the title, usually has three roles—leader, administrator, and presiding officer. **p. 173.**

2.   What are the fundamental qualities of the president as a leader?

     The president must have the ability to plan, ability to unite, and the courage to win. **p. 173.**

3.   List some important duties usually performed by the president as administrator?

     Acts as chief administrative officer and legal head of the organization; exercises supervision over the organization and all its activities and senior employees; represents and speaks for the organization; presides at business meetings; appoints committees as directed by the bylaws or the assembly; signs letters or documents necessary to carry out the will of the organization; and presides at meetings of the governing board. **p. 174.**

4.   A member moves to adjourn before some important business is conducted. What should the presiding officer do?

     If a member moves to adjourn and the presiding officer knows that there is important to be attended to, he should explain the situation to the member who may then withdraw the motion. If the member refuses to withdraw the motion to adjourn, the presiding officer should explain the business that needs attention before the vote on adjournment is taken. **p. 174.**

5.     What are the duties of the president as presiding officer?

The duties of the president as presiding officer are: to make sure that all members understand all proposals and what their effect will be if they are or are not adopted; should prevent improper conduct and should warn obstructionists who are using dilatory tactics; should encourage discussion; should expose parliamentary trickery; prevent railroading, and promptly rule out discussion of personalities; should be firm and decisive; and should have a working knowledge of parliamentary procedure and how to apply it. **p. 175.**

6.     What are the duties of the president-elect?

The president-elect assumes the duties of the president when that officer absent or is incapacitated, unless the bylaws provide something different. The president-elect also presides when necessary for the president to leave the chair temporarily. When acting in the place of the president at a meeting, the president-elect has all the powers, duties, responsibilities, and privileges that the president may exercise at a meeting. **p. 177.**

7.     What are the duties of the vice president?

There are two major duties of the vice president. When there is no president-elect, the vice president assumes the duties of the president in case of absence or incapacity of the president; and becomes president in the event of the death, resignation or permanent incapacity of the president unless the bylaws provide differently... The vice president is often assigned other duties through the bylaws. **p. 177.**

8.     What are the chief duties of the secretary?

The chief duties of the secretary are: take careful and accurate notes of the proceedings of meetings; prepare and certify the correctness of the minutes and enter them in the official minutes book or other means of storage; read the minutes or submit the proposed minutes to the organization for correction and approval; enter any corrections approved by the members into the minutes; record the approved minutes as the official minutes of the organization, with the date of their approval, signing them to attest to their validity; provide the presiding officer or the assembly with the exact wording of a pending motion or of one previously acted on; prepare a list of members and call the roll when directed by the presiding officer; read all papers, documents, or communications as directed by the presiding officer; bring to each meeting the minutes book, a copy of the bylaws, rules and policies; a list of the members, and a list of standing and special committees; and a copy of the adopted parliamentary authority adopted by the organization; search the minutes for information requested by officers or members; assist the presiding officer before each meeting in preparing a detailed agenda; preserve all records, reports, and official documents of the organization except those specifically assigned to the custody of others; prepare and send required notices of meetings and proposals; provide the chair of each special committee with a list of the committee members, a copy of the motion referred to the committee or the motion referring the subject to the committee, instructions, and other documents that may be useful; provide the chair of each standing committee with a copy of all proposals referred to it, instructions, or material that may be useful; sign official documents to attest to their authenticity; carry on the official correspondence of the organization as directed, except correspondence assigned to other officers; perform any additional duties required by applicable statutes. **pp. 178-179.**

9.  May an elected secretary propose a motion in a meeting while acting as secretary to the meeting?

    Yes. The elected secretary does not forfeit any rights of membership by reason of holding office and may propose motions and discuss and vote on all measures. **p. 179.**

10. What are the duties of the corresponding secretary?

The correspondence secretary conducts the official correspondence for the organization as directed by the president or board, answers official letters, and maintains a correspondence file. The corresponding secretary also communicates with outside organizations that have relationships with the organization. **p. 179.**

11. What are the duties of the treasurer?

The treasurer is responsible for the collection, safekeeping, and expenditures of all funds of the organization, and for keeping accurate financial records....The treasurer should report briefly on the finances at each membership and board meeting, answer any questions on financial matters, and submit a full report to the membership annually. **p. 180.**

12. What are the duties of the member parliamentarian?

The member parliamentarian should be a source of information on parliamentary procedure, but, like all parliamentarians, has no authority to make rulings and should act only as an advisor to the presiding officer. or to enforce them. **p. 181.**

13. What are the duties of the sergeant-at-arms?

The sergeant-at-arms, under direction of the presiding officer, helps to maintain order and decorum at meetings, acts as doorkeeper, directs the ushers, and is responsible for the comfort and convenience of the assembly. **p. 181.**

14. The bylaws restrict officers from serving more than one term in the same office. The president resigned and the vice president became president to complete the term. Is the new president restricted from being elected president in his own right?

No. Where there is a provision in the bylaws restricting the number of terms to which a member may be elected to a particular office, a member who fills a vacancy in that office for a partial term is not barred from being elected to a full term or terms, unless the bylaws provide otherwise. **p. 183.**

15.  How are vacancies filled?

A vacancy if filled by the same authority that selected the officer, director, or committee member unless the bylaws provide otherwise. **p. 184.**

16.  How is an officer or director removed from office?

Officers, directors, or committee members can be removed by the same authority that elected or appointed them. The power to select carries with it the power to remove. The bylaws should provide for procedures for removal or suspension. **p. 185.**

17.  What are the common valid causes for removal from office?

The common causes for removal from office are: continued, gross, or wilful neglect of the duties of the office; actions that intentionally violate the bylaws; failure to comply with the proper direction given by the assembly or the board; failure or refusal to disclose necessary information on matters of organization business; unauthorized expenditures, signing of checks, or misuse of organization funds; unwarranted attacks on any officer, member of the board of directors, or the board as a whole on an ongoing basis;; misrepresentation of the organization and its officers to outside persons; and conviction for a felony. **p. 185.**

18.  What conduct of an officer is NOT a valid reason for removal from office?

The following examples are not valid grounds for removal: poor performance as an officer due to lack of ability; negligence that is not gross or wilful; a tendency to create friction and disagreement; or mere unsuitability to hold office. **p. 186.**

This page intentionally left blank.

# CHAPTER 21
## Committees and Boards

1.  Why are committees important?

    Committees are important because they perform the bulk of the work of organizations. Members share in the work and responsibilities of their organization through committee service. Recommendations from the committee often become the final decisions of the organization. **p. 187.**

2.  What are the advantages of committees?

    The advantage of a committee is that it enables the work of the organization to be done more efficiently. Reasons are: greater freedom of discussion is possible; more time is available for each subject assigned to the committee; informal procedure is used in committee members; better use can be made of experts and consultants; delicate and troublesome questions may be considered privately; and hearings may be held giving members an opportunity to express their opinions. **pp. 187-188.**

3.  What is a standing committee?

    A standing committee is a committee that has a fixed term of office and does the work within its particular field that is assigned to it by the bylaws or referred to it by the organization, or the governing board. **p. 188.**

4.  Where are the specifics of the standing committee found?

    The name, number of members, quorum, method of selecting members, duties, term of office, and requirement for reports of each standing committee are often included in the bylaws. **p. 188.**

5.  What is a special committee sometimes called?

    A special committee is sometimes called an *ad hoc* committee, a task force, a commission, or anything else. **p. 188.**

6.    How are special committees classified?

Committees may be classified, according to the nature of their assignments, into committees primarily for deliberation and committees primarily for action. **p. 189.**

7.    If no committee chair is elected or appointed, how does the committee obtain a chair?

If no committee chair is elected or appointed, one may be selected by the committee from its own membership. If no chair is designated, the member first named calls the committee together and presides during the election of a chair. **pp. 189-190.**

8.    How are standing committee members selected?

Members of standing committees are appointed as directed in the bylaws, usually by the president with the approval of the governing board or assembly. It is often advisable for the president to consult a prospective committee chair regarding the selection of the other committee members and an incumbent committee chair regarding the appointment of a successor. **p. 190.**

9.    What are the rights of an ex officio member?

Unless the organization's governing documents provide otherwise, an ex officio member has all the rights, responsibilities and duties of other members of the committee, including the right to vote. Anyone who is not expected to be a regular working member of the committee should be designated as an advisory or consultant member instead of being given an ex officio status. **p. 190.**

10.    Should the president be an ex officio member of all committees?

*AIPSC* states, "for example, the president is often an ex officio member of all committees except the nominating committee...." **p. 190.** The president ... should not appoint any members of the nominating committee, serve on the committee, give the committee instructions, or take any part in its deliberations. **p. 162.**

11. Where are the powers, rights, and duties of a special committee found?

    The powers, rights, and duties of special committees should be provided for in the motions that create them or in the instructions given to them. **p. 191.**

12. Under whose control are all committees?

    Unless otherwise provided in the bylaws or in a resolution establishing a committee, all committees are under the direction and control of the authority that created or established them. Even an executive committee or board of directors has no powers and no duties except those delegated to it by the bylaws or by vote of the membership. **p. 191.**

13. How may a committee member be replaced?

    The members of a committee may be replaced by the appointing or electing authority. **p. 191.**

14. Can a committee represent the organization to an outside person or organization?

    Unless clearly authorized to do so, a committee cannot represent the organization to an outside person or organization. **p. 191.**

15. What information should the secretary furnish to each committee?

    The secretary is responsible for ensuring that each committee is furnished with specific instructions on the work it is expected to do, and with all helpful information that is in the possession of the organization. **p. 192.**

16. Who may attend committee meetings?

No officer, member, employee, or outside person has the right to attend any meetings of a committee except by invitation of the committee or by direction of the appointing body. If the committee wishes to invite a staff member, consultant, or other person, it may vote to do so. **pp. 192-193.**

17. What is the procedure in a committee meeting?

While committees preferably function with relaxed procedures, greater formality may be appropriate as the committee size increases, when the issues are complex or highly controversial, or when committee members have demonstrated an inability to work cooperatively. **p. 193.**

18. What is a committee hearing?

A committee hearing is a meeting at which a committee listens to the viewpoints of members, and sometimes experts, on the subject assigned to it. **p. 194.**

19. What is a governing board?

A governing board is usually a smaller elected group acting as the representatives of all the members to carry on the work of the organization during the intervals between meetings of the membership. The group is called the board of directors, executive board, board of trustees, or some other name meaning the governing board. **p. 195.**

20. Who generally composes the governing board of an organization?

A governing board of a voluntary organization is generally composed of the elected officers of the organization and of directors (trustees) elected by the membership. **p. 195.**

21. Where are the duties, responsibilities, and powers of the board of directors defined?

The duties, responsibilities, and powers of the board of directors should be clearly defined in the bylaws. **p. 195.**

22. What authority do members of a governing board have?

All members of a governing board share in a joint and collective authority, which exists and can be exercised only when the group is in session. Members of the board have no greater authority than any other member of the organization except when meeting as a board. **p. 196.**

23. How does an executive committee come into being?

The specific composition, powers, and duties of an executive committee should be provided for in the bylaws. **p. 196.**

24. Is it necessary to have a conflict of interest policy?

A director or officer of an organization may have business dealings with the organization, except when prohibited by the bylaws or by statutory law. The director or officer has both a legal and a moral duty to disclose any interest in such a transaction and must deal fairly with and in the best interests of the organization. . . . Many organizations adopt policies that define conflicts of interest and that provide the details of the expected or required conduct of officers and members with such conflicts. They also prescribe the procedures that are to be followed when the policies are violated. **pp. 196–197.**

This page intentionally left blank.

# CHAPTER 22
## Committee Reports and Recommendations

1.  What do committee reports usually include?

    Committee reports usually include: a statement of the question, subject, or work assigned to the committee, and any important instructions given to it; a brief explanation of how the committee carried out its work; a description of the work that the committee performed or, in the case of a deliberative or investigative committee, its findings and conclusions; and the committee's recommendations, usually in the form of main motions or resolutions. **p. 198.**

2.  Is the report of a committee valid if made without a meeting? Why?

    No. The report and the recommendations of a committee must be agreed on at a meeting of the committee. The committee members must have the opportunity to hear all the different viewpoints on the questions involved and to discuss them freely with each other. **p. 199.**

3.  How is a committee report presented?

    A committee report is presented by its chair or by some member of the committee designated to report. The reporting member may introduce the report with a brief explanation if necessary.

    In a convention or annual meeting of large organizations, committee reports usually are printed in advance and dio tributed to members by mail, electronically, or at the convention. In such case, the committee chair makes such explanatory statements as are needed and presents only the recommendations of the committee. **p. 200.**

4.  May a report be amended at the meeting when it is presented to the assembly?

A committee report cannot be amended except by the committee, since no one can make the committee say anything it does not wish to say. However, motions included as recommendations in the report, like all other motions, are subject to amendments and other action that would apply to any motion. **p. 201.**

5.   How is a committee report disposed of?

A committee report may be disposed of as follows: the report may be filed; the  subject and the report covering it may be referred back to the committee, or to another committee; it may be postponed to a more convenient time; or it may be adopted. Without a motion, the presiding officer may refer a financial report to the auditors; a financial report proposing future expenditures is treated as any other financial recommendation of a committee; a motion proposed by a committee is moved by the reporting committee member (usually the committee chair), or it is stated by the presiding officer. It does not require a second and is handled as any other main motion before the assembly, just as if it had been proposed from the floor and seconded. **pp. 201-202.**

6.   Is a committee report included in the minutes?

A committee report is not included in the body of the minutes unless the assembly votes that a brief summary be included. The report is usually handed to the secretary for filing in a special book or file reserved for committee reports. **p. 202.**

7.   What should be recorded in the minutes concerning a committee report?

Regarding committee reports, the minutes should record what reports were presented, by whom, the disposition of each report, and should record the page or file number where the particular report may be found. **p. 202.**

8.   When can a minority report be presented?

A minority report can be presented only immediately after the majority report. A minority has the right to present and read a report, even though a motion is pending to dispose of the majority report. **p. 203.**

9.    When may committee recommendations be presented?

Recommendations, which should be presented in the form of motions, may be acted on separately when they are presented with the committee report. Arter the presentation of the report, the chair of the committee reads the first recommendation of the committee and moves its adoption. **p. 203.**

10.   How should a committee recommendation be stated?

A committee recommendation should be stated in the form of a motion, which will allow the assembly to vote directly on the proposal itself, not on whether to agree or disagree with the recommendation of the committee. **p. 203.**

This page intentionally left blank.

# CHAPTER 23
## Conventions and Their Committees

1.    What is a convention?

A convention of an organization is a scheduled single meeting or a series of meetings that follow in close succession. The convention itself is regarded as a single meeting and should be provided for in the bylaws. During the convention, the voting members assemble to transact important business, offer educational sessions, social gatherings, and updates in the organization's particular field, exchange ideas and experiences, and to enjoy the fellowship of others who share a common interest. **p. 205.**

2.    Should voting delegates be instructed on how to vote?   Why?

It is usually not wise to instruct delegates to take specific action on items of business. The delegate should be permitted to weigh the pros and cons and to vote according to what appears to be the wisest course for the organization. **p. 206.**

3.    What is the responsibility of a delegate?

It is the delegate's responsibility to learn about the business to be transacted by the assembly and to act in the best interest of the organization as a whole. Delegates should to report to their constituents on the actions taken and explain the facts and arguments that resulted in the decisions that were made. **p. 206.**

4.    What are the duties of an alternate delegate?

The duties of an alternate delegate is to serve in place of the delegate who is unable to attend all or part of the meeting, learn the operation of the organization, assist in communicating the concerns of constituents to the assembly and communicate the business of the assembly to the constituents. **p. 206.**

5. What are the committees common to most conventions?

The committees common to most conventions are the credentials committee, the standing rules committee, and the program committee. **p. 206.**

6. What is the order in which these committees report?

The credentials committee reports first and is followed immediately by consideration and adoption of the reports of the standing rules committee and the program committee. **p. 207.**

7. When is the official list of delegates to a convention established?

It is established at the adoption of the credentials committee report. **p. 207.**

8. What does the credentials committee report contain?

The initial report of the credentials committee must include, at a minimum, the list of members entitled to vote. **p. 208.**

9. What does the rules committee report contain?

The rules committee recommends to the assembly a set of convention standing rules that define the operating procedure to be followed during the convention when it is desired to vary from, or add to, the provisions of the parliamentary authority. **p. 208.**

10. What vote is required to adopt the convention rules?

Unless otherwise provided in the bylaws or standing rules, the convention standing rules may be adopted by majority vote. **p. 209.**

11. What vote is required to suspend a convention standing rule?

A two-thirds vote is required to suspend a convention standing rule. **p. 209.**

12. Who gives permission to make subsequent changes to the agenda once it is adopted?

Once the agenda has been adopted, it is no longer under the control of the program committee and any subsequent changes must be made by the assembly itself, either by majority vote or general consent. p. **210.**

13. What are the duties of the teller's committee?

The teller's committee helps the presiding officer count standing and usually counts ballot votes, as well. It may be responsible for preparing ballots, ensuring ballot security, and issuing a report for all standing and ballot votes. **p. 210**.

14. What is a bylaws or governance committee often empowered to do?

The bylaws or governance committee may be empowered to approve the text of an amendment as written for submission to the assembly; reword the amendment to accomplish the intent of the maker in proper form used by the organization; combine several similar resolutions, with the permission of their proposers; and comment on and make recommendations regarding the proposed amendments. **p. 211.**

15. What limitation should be imposed on a bylaws or governance committee?

The committee should not be empowered to prevent the adoption of any proposed amendment by failing to report it to the voting body. **p. 211.**

This page intentionally left blank.

# CHAPTER 24
## Reference (or Resolutions) Committees

1.   What is the purpose of a reference committee?

     A reference committee typically is to arrive at recommendations for action on the items of business referred to it. It is usually done by studying the resolutions and background information before the convention and then hearing testimony from the membership. It recommends to the assembly what action should be taken on each proposal. **p. 212.**

2.   What is the composition of reference committee members?

     Reference committees should have at least three members and should be large enough to provide a reasonable cross section of the membership or convention delegates without becoming unwieldy. **p. 213.**

3.   Who appoints the reference committee members?

     The bylaws should designate how they will be appointed. Appointment by the president is customary in some organizations. **p. 213.**

4.   What are the advantages of a reference committee system?

     The system permits the assembly to deal with a large number of business items; each item of business may receive more in-depth consideration; informal consideration may be permitted; and the rules often allow members who might not otherwise have speaking opportunities to provide testimony. **pp. 213-214.**

5.   In organizations with large conventions, how are proposals for considerations submitted?

     Convention rules should provide a mechanism for the assembly to permit the introduction of late resolutions since business may arise that cannot be submitted before the designated deadline. . . . Depending on the bylaws, proposals in the form of motions or resolutions may be submitted by constituent organizations, committees or boards, officers, delegates and by individual members. The rules of the organization should identify how referral of resolutions should be made; the most common practice is for the presiding officer to make the referrals. **p. 214.**

6.   Who presides at the hearing of a reference committee?

The committee chair must conduct the hearing with a careful balance of the members' right to testify and the need to complete the hearings in a timely manner. **p. 215.**

7.   During the hearing, what restrictions, if any, are imposed at the hearing?

Depending on the number, complexity, and contentiousness of the resolutions assigned to a reference committee and the total time assigned for the hearings, it may be necessary to place some restrictions on the amount of time available for testimony on some or all items of business, on the duration of testimony by any given person, and on the number of times any one person may testify. **p. 215.**

8.   During the hearing, can motions to amend a resolution be made?

Motions are not in order during reference committee hearings. A member wishing to amend a resolution may, however, provide the reference committee with the language of the proposed amendment and urge the committee to recommend such an amendment, but the amendment is never formally introduced or considered at the hearing. **pp. 215-216.**

9.   In a reference committee hearing, may a member of the reference committee express opinions during the hearing?

No. The members of the committee should take care to conduct themselves impartially. Reference committee members are permitted to ask questions to clarify the testimony of a member or to obtain additional information on the matter at hand. **p. 216.**

10. After a hearing, what does the reference committee do?

After the hearings have been concluded, the reference committee deliberates on its recommendations for action on each item of business that has been referred to it. **p. 217.**

In a closed meeting, the full committee approves all recommendations for action. The committee chair often drafts any explanatory language. When this is done, the committee should reconvene to give approval of the full final report, including the final wording of explanations. The report should then be signed by all members of the reference committee. **p. 220.**

11. How is the report of the reference committee given?

Typically, the reference committee develops a written report with its recommendations on each item of business referred to it. Recommendations may include: approval or adoption; disapproval; amendment and approval as amended; referral; or postponement (rarely used). It may also make an explanation of the reasons for the committee's recommendations on each proposal. **p. 218.**

12. What requirements are necessary regarding the wording of reference committee recommendations?

The resolutions should be worded in the affirmative and be clear and unambiguous in their meaning. The resolved clauses represent the action to be taken and should be complete in themselves ("stand alone") without reference to any "whereas" clauses in the resolution. Care should be taken to avoid wording that will result in uncertainty as to what action will be taken as a result of adopting the resolution. **p. 219.**

13. What is a consent agenda and how is it used in a conven-

tion?

The consent agenda is usually composed of all the items on which the reference committee feels its recommendations are likely to be accepted by the assembly without objection. Most organizations allow any noncontroversial items to be included on the consent agenda, no matter what the reference committee's recommendation for action may be. **p. 220.**

14.   When should a priority agenda be utilized?

If the available meeting time is less than might be desirable, a parliamentary tool called the "priority agenda" may be employed. This is a method of considering important items of business before the remainder of the agenda is considered. **pp. 221-222.** Also see **p. 121.**

15.   What is the purpose of the motion to adopt in-lieu-of?

The purpose is to allow the assembly to arrive at the final action with fewer votes. Multiple resolutions on similar subject matter are commonly received and referred to the reference committee, which may wish to propose a single substitute that takes the best features of each of these multiple resolutions, based on testimony and other background materials and to recommend its adoption as a substitute for each and all of the "underlying" resolutions. **p. 222.**

By using adopt in-lieu-of, the assembly can adopt a single main motion in place of a number of similar main motions. **p. 39.**

16.   What is the process for using the motion to adopt in-lieu-of?

The reference committee recommends that its motion, which is fully stated, be adopted in lieu of other resolutions, specifically identifying those to be replaced (usually by resolution number). With the adoption of the adopt in-lieu-of motion, the underlying resolutions are not acted on directly, but are considered moot. **p. 224.**

17. What happens when the adopt in-lieu-of motion is defeated?

If the adopt in-lieu-of motion fails, no options have been eliminated. If the adopt in-lieu of motion proposed by the reference committee is not adopted, the presiding officer announces that it is not adopted and that any member may, if he or she wishes, propose the adoption of any one of the underlying resolutions in lieu of the other remaining resolutions. **p. 224.**

18. Does the reference committee take the place of a vigilant and knowledgeable membership?

No, every member must be vigilant, knowledgeable of each item of business, and prepared to lead the assembly in the decision-making process if he or she disagrees with the recommendation of the reference committee and thinks there is a reasonable probability that the assembly might concur. **p. 226.**

This page intentionally left blank.

# CHAPTER 25
## Minutes

1.  What is the importance of minutes?

    Minutes are the legal history and record of official actions of an organization. The accuracy of the minutes is essential. Auditors depend on the minutes as proof of financial actions authorized by the organization and by courts as evidence of actions taken. **p. 227.**

2.  What are the responsibilities of the secretary?

    The secretary is responsible for recording all actions taken at business meetings, preparing proposed (draft) minutes, recording any corrections, and certifying the official minutes by signing them when they have been approved by the organization. The secretary is responsible for the completeness and accuracy of the proposed minutes. **p. 227.**

    The secretary is the custodian of the official minutes. **p. 228.**

3.  Who can inspect the minutes?

    The minutes of a general membership meeting or a convention are open to inspection by members of the organization. Except when the bylaws or rules indicate otherwise, minutes of a board or committee meeting are available only to members of the board or committee. In the case of some incorporated organizations or public bodies, the law may require that the minutes be available to members or to the public. **p. 228.**

4.  What is the appropriate format that minutes must use?

    The format of minutes should meet several specific objectives: the minutes should be easy to access and easy to review for pertinent actions. The format should be easily duplicated from meeting to meeting and easy-to-read. The complexity of the organization's meeting may determine the format chosen. **p. 228.**

5. When should the minutes be prepared?

The secretary should prepare the draft minutes as soon as possible after a meeting. **p. 228.**

6. Can any member request to see the minutes of a closed meeting (executive session)?

No, the minutes of a closed meeting are available only to members who attended the closed meeting or who would be authorized to attend. **p. 228.**

7. Are minutes kept in a committee meeting and if so, for what purpose?

Yes, committee minutes are less formal and generally brief, but in some cases they may be more detailed than those of meetings of the organization because they often serve as the basis for the committee's report. **p. 229.**

8. What should minutes contain?

The minutes contain a record of all actions and proceedings in the meeting but not a record of the discussion. **p. 229.** Note that, **pp. 229 and 230** contain an exhaustive list of what the minutes contain.

9. What should minutes NOT contain?

Minutes should not contain: discussion; procedural motions except when they affect future action; names of seconders; personal opinions, personal interpretations, or comments; descriptive or judgemental phrases; criticism of members except when action on a motion to censure or reprimand a member. Motions of thanks, gratitude, or commendation generally appear in the form of a courtesy resolution. **pp. 230-231.**

10. How are corrections made to the minutes?

The presiding officer assumes a motion for the approval of the minutes and asks, "Are there any corrections to the minutes?" When corrections are suggested they are usually approved by general consent. If there is an objection to the proposed correction, the presiding officer should take a majority vote to approve the change proposed. **p. 231.**

11.  When may minutes be corrected?

At the appropriate place in the order of business, the presiding officer assumes the motion for approval of the proposed minutes, by stating "Are there any corrections to the minutes?" **p. 231.**

If, however, an error is discovered at a later time, the error may be corrected by the assembly, regardless of the lapse of time, by a majority vote. **p. 232.**

12.  When should a minutes approving committee be used?

If an organization that does not meet often, it is important to have a committee on minutes to which all proposed minutes are referred to correction and approval. An organization that does not meet at least every three months should have a committee to approve the minutes of the meeting. The authority for a minutes approval committee should be included in the organization's governing documents or granted by adoption of a motion. **p. 232.**

13.  What are the various forms of published minutes?

There are several forms of published minutes, including those printed for distribution, e-mailed to the members, and placed on a website or in the organization's official publication. Minutes are generally limited to the substantive action items taken at a meeting. If any discussion is included, it must cover both sides of the issue without prejudice. **p. 233.**

14.  What must be considered to ensure proper retention of the electronic minutes?

Signed minutes should be maintained with the same security measures as other legal documents of the organization. If various versions of electronic files of minutes are created as a result of corrections, the versions should be clearly identified, with the correct version always identified as "final" in some way and with draft versions deleted as appropriate. At regular intervals, a hard copy or a retrievable electronic copy of the approved minutes should be kept in a safe location. **p. 234.**

15. Can the minutes be approved as distributed with the motion to "dispense with the reading of the minutes"?

A motion to "dispense with the reading of the minutes" is confusing. If the intent is to delay the reading until later in the meeting, the motion should be "That the reading of the minutes be postponed (time)." If the intent is that the minutes not be read aloud, and that the distributed printed version be approved, the motion should be, "That the minutes be approved as distributed." **p. 234.**

16. What are the shortcuts that a secretary may use for taking minutes during a meeting?

The use of a minutes template is a format of an organization's minutes that is used by the secretary to prepare an initial version of the minutes prior to the meeting. He or she has only to "fill in the blanks." The common elements are the type of meeting; the location; the presiding officer; the presence of the secretary; call to order; any routine opening ceremonies; the quorum statement; names of all members listed for a roll call may also be formatted before the meeting begins. **p. 235.**

17. What is the general purpose of an action log?

The action log is a system of recording actions taken, but which is separate from the minutes. It allows the organization to quickly review previous decisions. **p. 236.**

# CHAPTER 26
## Governing Documents: Charters, Bylaws, and Rules

1.    What are the types of governing documents of an organization?

      An organization may be governed by statutes, a charter, a constitution, bylaws, or standing rules or by two or more of these. **p. 237.**

2.    What are the two types of charters?

      The two types of charters are charters of incorporation from government and charters from a parent organization. **p. 237.**

3.    Who approves amendment of a charter granted by the government?

      Most state corporation statutes provide the method for amending the corporate charter. No amendment to the charter or articles of incorporation is effective until it has been approved in the manner prescribed by law and also by the governmental authority that granted the charter. **p. 238.**

4.    If the constitution and bylaws are two separate documents, what should each address?

      In an unincorporated association, the constitution should address those issues usually addressed in a corporate charter, such as name, purpose, and requirements for tax-exempt status. The bylaws supplement these fundamental provisions and are usually easier to amend. **p. 238.**

5.    What is the function of bylaws?

      The function of the bylaws of an organization is to define the privileges secured and the duties assumed by the members and to set up a framework of the organization. An organization has the right to adopt such bylaws as the members may agree upon, so long as they are not contrary to the public policy, the law, or a higher level governing document. **p. 239.**

6.   When drafting the bylaws, what level of detail is needed?

The bylaws contain all the details necessary to make the organization function. Administrative details are enumerated in the standing rules. Bylaws are written to meet the needs of the particular organization. **p. 239.**

7.   What vote is required to adopt original bylaws?

A majority vote is required to adopt the original bylaws. **p. 240.**

8.   When do bylaws go into effect?

They go into effect immediately with the announcement of the vote adopting them unless the motion to adopt provides that the bylaws, or some portion or provision in them, are not affective until a later date. **p. 240.**

9.   What specific requirements should be in the bylaws concerning amending bylaws?

It is good practice for an organization to include in its bylaws specific requirements that cover the following: how and by whom amendments to bylaws may be initiated and proposed; the form in which proposed amendments should be stated; the date before which proposed amendments must be received by the organization; the required notice to members of proposed amendments; and the vote required to adopt the amendment. **pp. 240-241.**

10.   What is a simple method of stating a proposed amendment?

In many local groups, any member may rise while new business is being considered and offer an amendment to the bylaws simply by stating the proposed amendment and giving a copy of it to the secretary. **p. 241.**

11. How are bylaws amendments considered?

At a meeting or convention, when the time arrives for consideration of the proposed amendments, the chair or some other member of the bylaws or reference committee reads the first proposed amendment as it is stated in the notice and moves its adoption. Since a proposed amendment to the bylaws is a specific main motion *to amend a previous action,* it may be amended, and an amendment to that amendment is also in order. **p. 242.**

12. What vote is required on amendments to bylaws?

A vote required to amend the bylaws should be stated in the bylaws. If *AIPSC* is the parliamentary authority and the bylaws are silent on the vote required to amend or revise the bylaws, it requires a majority of the legal votes cast. **p. 244.**

13. What is a revision of bylaws?

A revision of the bylaws is the simplest method when it is necessary to amend portions of the bylaws resulting in the extensive changes. A revision proposes, in effect, a new set of bylaws, and the revision is presented and considered in the same manner as an amendment of the bylaws. **p. 244.**

14. What vote is required to adopt a revision to the bylaws?

A revision requires the same vote and advance notice that is required to amend the bylaws. **p. 244.**

15. Who has the final say on the interpretation of bylaws?

The final decision on an interpretation of the bylaws and rules, when they are ambiguous, rests with the membership, unless the bylaws assign this authority to another body. **p. 245.**

16. What are standing rules?

Standing rules are those rules that add to or vary from the rules of parliamentary law as stated in their parliamentary authority. They are intended to stand until revoked. Standing rules cover points of lesser importance than those contained in the bylaws. **p. 245.**

17. How might an organization cite the *American Institute of Parliamentarians Standard Code of Parliamentary Procedure* in its bylaws as the organization's parliamentary authority?

It may be stated as follows: "In all matters not covered by its constitution, bylaws, and standing rules, this organization shall be governed by the current edition of *American Institute of Parliamentarians Standard Code of Parliamentary Procedure.*" **p. 246.**

18. Where should detailed procedures be placed?

Detailed procedures should not be included in the bylaws as they will add length and confusion. These procedures adopted by an organization are called *adopted procedures*. They should be classified under a suitable heading – such as "Convention Credentials Committee Procedures." **p. 246.**

19. Bylaws define the structure of an organization. What do policies define?

Policies define the beliefs and philosophy of an organization and like the bylaws are equally binding. They are often as important in determining the actions of an organization as the bylaws or other rules. Policies are usually formulated to meet recurring problems that come up for decision. **p. 247.**

20. If a proposal is contrary to an adopted policy of the organization, how should the presiding officer deal with it?

It should not be considered unless the policy is first amended to permit such a proposal. **p. 247.**

# CHAPTER 27
## Finances

1.  What are some considerations needed when developing an accounting system?

    A good system for controlling finances saves time and money. If an organization expects to receive gifts or solicit contributions for specific causes, it should make sure to comply with laws regarding solicitation of funds (which may apply wherever funds are solicited, and not just in the jurisdiction of incorporation or the location of the organization's headquarters). **p. 249.**

2.  What should the treasurer's report contain?

    At each regular meeting, the treasurer should give a brief report or summary of the organization's revenue and expenses and call attention to any unusual items. The treasurer should make a complete report annually. All members should receive copies of this report, the auditor's certification, and any recommendations made by the treasurer or auditor. **p. 249.**

3.  How is the treasurer's report dealt or disposed with?

    The report should be filed for future reference. **p. 249.**

4.  What are the usual duties of a finance committee?

    If an organization has a finance committee, the committee should report at least quarterly, giving a realistic picture of the financial situation and problems of the organisation and any contemplated proposals or plans involving finances. **p. 249.**

5.  Who selects the auditor?

    The auditor should be selected by vote of the governing board, the audit committee, or the membership. **p. 250.**

6. Which profession is authorized by law to express professional and independent opinions on the financial statements of an organization?

Certified and licensed public accountants are authorized by law to do so. **p. 250.**

7. The auditor's report is an opinion on the treasurer's report. What are the two types of report that the auditors provide?

The auditor when engaged may be requested to provide a *short-form* report or a *long-form* report. The standard short-form report consists of two paragraphs expressing the auditor's opinion on the financial statements. The long-form report, in addition to the contents of the short-form report, describes and explains in detail the significant items in the financial statements. **p. 250.**

8. What are some financial safeguards that an organization can adopt?

The adoption of a budget; the requirement of authorization for purchases; strict supervision of officers, committees, or employees who collect or expend funds or incur financial obligations; separation of the members or employees recording incoming funds and those recording outgoing expenditures; an annual audit, and a blanket bond (insurance) covering all members and employees who have access to organization's funds. **p. 251.**

9. What is a budget?

A budget is an estimate only of revenues and expenses. It is a financial guide. Some groups require the authorization of the governing board or the membership for any expenditure in excess of budgeted amounts or any expenditure not included in the budget. **p. 251.**

10. Who should approve unusual or particular large expenditures?

Some organizations provide that such expenditures require authorization by vote of the board of directors or of the membership. **p. 251.**

This page intentionally left blank.

# CHAPTER 28
## Types of Organizations

1.    What is the difference between a temporary and a permanent organization?

A temporary organization may exist for a few meetings or a single meeting. It dissolves automatically as soon as the members accomplish the purpose for which they organized. A permanent organization is one formed with the intention of functioning over a considerable period of time, indefinitely, in perpetuity, or until it is dissolved. **p. 252.**

2.    What are some of the common forms of nonprofit and business entities?

Most nonprofit membership organizations choose to organize either as unincorporated associations or as corporations. Nonprofit corporations may be organized as membership corporations or as board-only corporations. Business entities include partnerships and business corporations. Some nonprofits, typically those without individual members, and many businesses choose to organize as trusts, or as limited liability companies.  pp. **252-253.**

3.    Unincorporated nonprofit entities that are rather loosely structured and operate only under a set of their own governing documents are termed *unincorporated associations*. **p. 254**.

4.    What are the chief advantages of incorporation?

The chief advantages of incorporation are: the organization holds a charter from government and operates under the guidance and protection of the applicable laws governing corporations; the purposes of the organization and the powers necessary to carry out these purposes have legal recognition; the individual or member groups are able to work with greater effectiveness and scope by pooling their resources and efforts; the process for dissolution is generally more difficult and the organization exists permanently until dissolved; the corporation is recognized as an legal entity and thus can do business and hold property of any kind in its own right; officers, directors, and members are free from personal liability for debts of the organization; and the name and seal of the organization are legally protected. **pp. 255-256.**

5. What are the statutory requirements if a nonprofit association is incorporated?

   The members should be aware that in addition to having their bylaws and practices comply with their corporate charter; they also must comply with applicable corporation codes. **p. 257.**

6. What is the main requirement of a nonprofit corporation?

   The main requirement of the nonprofit corporation is that any income or profit of the organization must be used solely to carry out its legal purpose and cannot be distributed as profit to its members. **p. 258.**

7. If a nonprofit organization receives profit incidental to its operation, how must that profit be used?

   Incidental profit must be used for the purposes for which the organization exists. **p. 258.**

8. May an unincorporated nonprofit organization qualify as a tax-exempt entity?

   Yes, whether incorporated or not, the organization may be treated by federal, state, territorial, or provincial government as a *tax-exempt entity*. **p. 258.**

# CHAPTER 29
## Rights of Members and of Organizations

1.  What is the relationship between a member and the organization?

    When a member joins an organization, an implicit relationship is formed between the member and the organization. The current charter, bylaws, and other rules of the organization are a part of the implicit contract binding both the members and the organization. **p. 259.**

2.  What are the fundamental rights of members?

    All members have the following fundamental rights under common parliamentary law, subject only to any specific limitations contained in the bylaws: to be notified of meetings; to attend meetings; to make motions; to speak on debatable matters; to vote; to run for office, nominate and elect officers and directors; to propose and vote on amendments to governing documents; to insist on the enforcement of the rules of the organization and of parliamentary law; to resign from office or from the organization itself; to remain in the organization even when on the losing side of a particular proposition; to have a fair hearing before expulsion or other penalties are applied; to receive or have right to inspect copies of all documents of authority, minutes, or other official records of the organization; to exercise any other rights or privileges given to the members by law, or by the bylaws, or by the rules of the organization. **p. 260.**

3.  What is the definition of a member in good standing?

    A member in good standing can usually exercise all the rights of membership. The term has some basis in law, but each organization should provide its own definition, which should clearly describe the events that can lead to a loss of good standing and the particular conditions, if any, that must be met to maintain good standing; the consequences of the loss of good standing; and the conditions that must be met to restore good standing. **p. 261.**

4.  List some of the fundamental rights of an organization.

    An organization has the following rights which are exercised by the decision of the organization: to carry out its mission and to exercise any of the rights or authority granted it by law; to change its purposes, if permitted by law and its charter, to merge with another organization, or to dissolve; to establish eligibility requirements and procedures governing the admission of members, and to grant or refuse membership according to its adopted rules and within the law; to establish and to amend, through changes in its bylaws, the rights, privileges, and obligations of its members either by extension or by limitation; to delegate authority, within legal limits, to officers, directors, committees, and employees; to select its officers, directors, and committee members and to suspend or remove them as prescribed by the bylaws or the law; to discipline or expel members, directors, and officers in accordance with its bylaws and within the law; and to purchase and hold property and to defend against or enter into litigation in its own name, if permitted by applicable law. **p. 262.**

5.  How should the individual member regard his rights in relation to the rights of other members and of the organization?

    Although each member has certain membership rights, in order for the member to assert these rights, the member must choose the proper time and forum. The member must follow the proper procedures. For example, a member has the right to have correct procedure followed; however the demand for this enforcement must be made in a timely and appropriate manner. **p. 262.**

6.  How do the rights of others and of the organization surpass the rights of the individual?

The individual member's rights gives way to the organization's right to set its own rules. If the rights of an individual member conflicts with the rights of the majority of the assembly, the rights of the majority ultimately must prevail unless the governing documents protect the minority. **p. 263.**

7.  Procedures for the discipline and expulsion of members should be included _in the bylaws_. **p. 263**.

8.  When is termination of membership justified?

    An organization has the inherent power to expel a member because of violation of an important duty to the organization, a breach of a fundamental rule or principle of the organization, or for any violation stated in the bylaws as grounds for expulsion. **p. 263.**

    An organization has the implied power to expel a member for violation of duties as a citizen. For example, a member may be expelled upon being convicted of a criminal offense that would discredit the organization. **p. 264.**

9.  What are the essential steps for imposing severe discipline or expelling a member?

    The primary requisites for expulsion proceedings are due notice and a fair hearing. The essential steps for imposing severe discipline or expelling a member are: charges in affidavit form stating the alleged violations and preliminary proof should be filed with the secretary; a disinterested committee should investigate the charges thoroughly and promptly, and if it decides a hearing is warranted, it should set the date for the hearing and notify the secretary; the secretary should send the accused member a registered or certified letter at least 15 days before the date of the hearing; a hearing should be held at either a closed membership meeting or by a hearing committee; the hearing committee should within reasonable time make findings of fact, recommend a decision, and send a copy of the recommended decision and findings of fact to the accused member and to the secretary; and if the member is found guilty of the charges, a penalty should be recommended to the membership meeting. **pp. 264-265.**

10. When does a member have the right to resign?

   A member has the absolute right to resign from an organization at any time. **p. 265.**

11. When does a resignation become effective?

   A resignation becomes effective immediately, unless the resigning member specifies some future time. No acceptance of the resignation is necessary to make it effective unless the bylaws say otherwise. **p. 265.**

12. Can an officer or director who has resigned either orally or in writing resume office because of a change of mind?

   If the resignation is intended to become effective immediately, it cannot be withdrawn. However, a resignation that specifies it is effective at some future date may be withdrawn until it is accepted, or until the effective date of the resignation. **p. 266.**

# CHAPTER 30
## Staff and Consultants

1. To whom is the executive director responsible?

   The executive director, executive secretary, executive officer, chief executive officer, administrative officer, or manager is usually chosen by the governing board or executive committee and is responsible to the selecting body. **p. 267.**

2. What other professional individuals may an organization find advantageous to hire?

   A full-time chief financial officer who is also an accountant, the services of a management and business consultant, an attorney, and a parliamentarian. **p. 268-269.**

3. What are the situations in which an attorney's services are essential?

   The attorney's services are essential on all important legal matters. For example, the following would require legal help: incorporating the organization; creating a foundation; developing contracts; taking disciplinary actions; pursuing litigation; preparing legal documents relating to employment, mergers, consolidations, dissolution, purchase or sale of property, and any other major purchases. **p. 269.**

4. What are the duties of the parliamentarian?

   In general, the duty of a parliamentarian is to aid and advise the president, governing board, committees, members, and staff. **p. 269.**

   At a meeting or convention, the parliamentarian advises the presiding officer on procedures. If requested by the presiding officer, the parliamentarian may make explanations to the assembly. The parliamentarian cannot make rulings, but only advises the presiding officer who makes the rulings. The parliamentarian is not an advocate of causes or a representative of any group within the organization, but is retained to help the members do what they wish to do and to find a valid way of accomplishing, if possible, the legitimate purposes of the organization. **p. 269.**

5.   Under whose direction does the parliamentarian usually work?

The parliamentarian is usually chosen by, and works under, the direction of the presiding officer. **p. 269.**

6.   Where does the parliamentarian usually sit during a convention?

At a meeting or convention, the parliamentarian should sit next to the presiding officer. **p. 269.**

7.   Under what circumstances might a parliamentarian preside?

There may be times when it may be advantageous for the parliamentarian to preside over the business portion of a meeting or convention or when a part of the meeting may be controversial and the assembly would welcome a neutral party to preside. Such action requires the permission of the assembly, usually granted by general consent. However, only those duties associated with the business of the meeting are assumed by the parliamentarian. **pp. 270-271.**

CPSIA information can be obtained
at www.ICGtesting.com
Printed in the USA
LVHW062258060721
692054LV00020B/501